HEARTS OF STEEL

HEARTS OF STEEL

The Warship Paintings of Paul Wright

First published in Great Britain in 2009

British Library Cataloguing-in-Publication Data
A CIP record for this title is available from the British Library

ISBN 978 1 906690 05 2

HALSTAR
Halsgrove House,
Ryelands Industrial Estate,
Bagley Road, Wellington, Somerset TA21 9PZ
Tel: 01823 653777   Fax: 01823 216796
email: sales@halsgrove.com

An imprint of Halstar Ltd, part of the halsgrove group of companies
Information on all Halsgrove titles is available at: www.halsgrove.com

Printed and bound by Grafiche Flaminia, Italy

DEDICATION

For Dan S. Somekh
True patron and friend

FOREWORD

As artists we cannot choose what images haunt us from our earliest childhood, images which we are sometimes fated to spend the remainder of our lives mediating through our art. They may come from a particular place, a landscape or a city; or the human face and body; or indeed be sharks or cows. In my own case they are sailing ships. And in the case of Paul Wright, they are iron and steel warships.

There are few more impressive things of human construction than a warship. Here is a huge self-contained mobile structure, to all appearances an autonomous machine, designed to be pitched in battle against other machines. It is a brilliant piece of engineering, usually one of the most technically advanced creations of its day, which can nevertheless be seen at a glance as an isolated object, compact, shaped, attached to nothing else around it. At the same time it is wholly human, a manned fortress containing a microcosm of human society, a town at sea, with all its hierarchies and its characters, its history, its crimes and glories, even its own personality. Paul succeeds in conveying something of all these elements in his paintings – the often brooding atmosphere, the massive size, the infinitely complex detail, the power both of the ship and of its other constant enemy, the sea. He is clearly awestruck by his subject, and like any good artist communicates what he feels to the viewer.

I have known Paul's work for many years – we started out along the same path together, painting illustrations for book jackets, I painting the sailing ships while he painted the ships of steel, each occasionally trespassing on the other's territory. But it was not just to make a living that we settled on these subjects. Ships and their stories were our whole inspiration, and we would have painted them regardless, tiresome company to our friends and relatives, whether or not anyone had paid us to do so. It gives me particular pleasure that Paul has invited me to contribute the foreword to this book. No one has explored his subject more thoroughly, with a more passionate dedication, than Paul Wright. This book is the distillation of his art, and a rare treat.

Geoff Hunt
September 2008

ACKNOWLEDGEMENTS

There have been many people who have helped me in my career over the years and more recently in the production of this book. I have been blessed with support and helpful advice from friends, family and colleagues including Bill, Caroline and Bernard Bowen-Davies, Fred Phillips, Peter and Annie Podmore, John and Lesley Butterworth.

Ian Ballentyne of *Warship International*, J.Russell Jinishian of the Jinishian Gallery, Julian Thomas of Art Marine, Charles Mayes of Marine Artists Ltd, Richard Cosby of Maritime Prints and Originals, Ron Feltham, Brian Love, Trevor Hewett, Peter Woods, Simon Butler of Halsgrove Publishing, Duncan Forbes, Ameet Hindoucha and John Wood. I must also acknowledge the kind help and real photographic expertise of Niall Buchannan of Kingston University and Michel Foucard de Fontefiguieres who have contributed so much to the production of this book.

Also I would like to thank Geoff Hunt, Past President of the Royal Society of Marine Artists for his kind and generous foreword to this book and my family, especially Patrick and Frances Wright whose love has sustained me throughout my life and work. Finally I must give a special thanks to Dan S. Somekh of Boca Raton, Florida, whose help and support has made this book possible and to whom it is gratefully dedicated.

At the time of going to press, all the paintings in this book are for sale unless otherwise indicated.

p.wright1@btinternet.com

INTRODUCTION

If any single event can be said to have changed anyone's life then a hot July day in 1959 certainly changed mine. The event was a school trip to Portsmouth Naval Dockyard arranged for us ten-year-old-schoolboys by a kindly father who as a serving naval officer in the navy laid on a day devoid of the usual castles and cathedrals and the other staples of school history trips. Instead we visited H.M.S. *Victory* in the morning and were then escorted to a motor launch for a tour of the dockyard, prior to the high spot of the visit. Our tour guide, an unsmiling one-eyed one-armed latter day Nelson provided with us with a perfunctory commentary interposed with such commands as 'Don't look at this, don't look at that' or 'that's a military secret, don't look at it!' so being schoolboys we looked at torpedoes being lowered into submarines and the latest cruiser (*Tiger*) taking on ammunition and stores.

Then our launch rounded the bend and there before us like a block of white flats set on an azure mirror-like sea lay H.M.S. *Vanguard*, the last and largest British battleship, the sheer size and grace of her simply took my breath away. Not even the tea and curled up sandwiches they served us could spoil this first impression of might, power and tradition, although standing at the jack staff and looking back across the broad deck I was not to know that I was looking at a ship that was already an anachronism, a once proud fleet flagship already condemned and slated for scrapping the following year.

Yet only twenty years before, the battleship was the major capital ship, the possession of which mirrored a nation's success and ambition. During three periods of the twentieth century the great powers tried to out-build each other with larger and larger battleships and heavy cruisers, and even smaller nations joined in, bankrupting themselves in the process. The noted historian Professor Arthur Marder described the battleship as 'Yesterdays deterrent', a deterrent, unlike today's missiles hidden in silos or submarines, designed to be the very visible protector of their respective countries interests. With their huge size, massive guns and armour plating, the dreadnought battleship was the ultimate expression of a nation's prestige and power. When battleships were launched the event was a public occasion, filmed and photographed; christened by Kaisers, Kings, Presidents and Dictators, the propaganda value of such celebrations was perceived as having almost as much value as the ships themselves.

As each great vessel begat an even greater one, their vital statistics were eagerly studied by naval attachés and schoolboys alike. The greater the ship, the greater the projection of her nation's virility. Children's games and cigarette cards promoted the cult of the 'super' battleship, naval leagues and clubs sprang up all over the world to press for more and bigger ships, and when such vessels visited foreign ports, carnivals, public holidays and spies attended their arrival. Battleships were big national business.

Only one country built their latest battleships in secret. The Japanese navy, the third largest in the inter-war period, went to obsessive and extraordinary lengths to hide the construction of the two greatest dreadnoughts the world has ever seen. The gigantic *Yamato* and *Musashi* were not built as deterrents but for the war the Japanese knew they would have to fight in order to extend their empire. When that war ended in their country's defeat, the Japanese secret police destroyed all records that the, by now, sunken ships had ever existed.

Thus the two giants entered the world of mythology, the 'Holy Grail' of battleships for the Japanese who even created a

fantasy comic book built around their resurrection and rebirth as 'Space Battleships' forever sailing the stella oceans. And if that is not enough, a *Yamato* museum has been created at Kure where the original ship was built. Part museum and part shrine, this museum houses the largest model ship ever built. The size of a least two double-decker buses, this recreated *Yamato* has recently been eclipsed by a Japanese film company who in their epic 'Last Battle of the *Yamato*' built a full sized replica from the deck up. The resulting movie has been one of the most successful in Japanese cinema history.

However, battleship legends do not only exist in Japan. The image of the 'Mighty *Hood*', old and somewhat frail, yet one of the most beautiful creations of the shipbuilders' art, steaming into battle against the modern, massively efficient *Bismarck* and being literally blown to atoms with her entire crew, save three, in under two minutes, is both majestic and terrible. This graceful battle-cruiser was in many Britons' eyes the Royal Navy personified, and her loss was as the loss of an old and dear friend. Today there is are several websites celebrating H.M.S. *Hood* and more books have been written about her than any other comparable ship.

As befits their purpose, warships have always been invested with drama, both momentous and tragic. Even the victory at Trafalgar seemed to require the death of Nelson to complete the symmetry of glory. Consider the fate of Sir Christopher Cradock who sallied forth to meet his destruction at the hands of Admiral Graf von Spee's squadron off the coast of Chile in 1914. We forget the tactical errors he may have made and the unnecessary sacrifice of the two elderly cruisers and all their crews that was the result of the Battle of Coronel. We do remember a brave man facing impossible odds and certain doom yet standing to his duty. We may question the tactics but we remember the glory. And that glory also belongs to his opponent who shortly afterwards met his

own nemesis off the Falkland Islands, the result of his own faulty tactics and hubris. Yet his name and those of his sons who served under him in this battle now have their honoured place in the Valhalla of naval heroes. The names of their famous ships, *Scharnhorst* and *Gneisenau* lived on to grace two equally-famous German warships in the Second World War. And surely this Valhalla also holds an honoured place for the master of U.S.S *Johnston*, Ernest E. Evans, who with two other destroyers faced down an entire Japanese battlefleet off Samar Island in 1944 and whose sacrifice helped save a fleet of small American carriers from almost certain destruction. The ships and the men may have long gone but the legends, the sacrifice and the heroism remain..

PAINTING THE SHIPS

For the marine artist naval history falls into two distinct periods which could be called 'wooden walls' and 'steam and steel'. Up until H.M.S. *Warrior* of 1851, the warship had not essentially changed since Elizabethan times. Any one of Sir Francis Drake's sailors would have been quite at home on Nelson's *Victory*, the technology was still wood, canvas and rope. The advance of science and especially metallurgy after 1851 transformed the warship completely. A warship's useful life in Nelson's time was usually about 50 years before she rotted away. By 1900, with the speed of technology outstripping shipbuilding and naval tactics, the useful life of a warship was no more than 15 years. This presents the painter of battleships, cruisers and destroyers with certain problems. As the speed of technological change altered the appearance of these ships several times over their service lives, it is important for the painter to fix the work in a certain time to

take account of any changes that may have taken place. That is not to say that the artist wishes the viewer to count every rivet in order to claim the veracity of the painting, it is only necessary that they believe that the rivets are there and that they are certainly in the right place. After all, when we look at buildings we don't want to remember the scaffolding used in their construction, however if the builder tried to construct a building without scaffolding, their job would be almost impossible and the building would probably fall down.

By the same token, the marine artist needs to have some knowledge of how the ship was built in the same way that a knowledge of the skeleton and muscles in the human body is necessary to draw the human figure. So it is with any structure, and especially with ships; failure to understand this will lead to the dreaded 'rubber ship' syndrome, the maritime version of Churchill's famous 'Boneless Wonder'.

DRAMA

The first thing to paint is the sky, taking account of the position of the sun and the wind direction for flag and smoke direction. The overall colour of the sky is reflected in the sea and this in turn affects that of the ship. A surprising number of painters have failed to understand this, throwing their pictures into confusion with mysterious science-fiction lighting, and shadow effects falling all over the place. The next question is what is the ship doing? How heavy is it, is it turning, pitching, listing etc. Careful observation will show that heavy ships do not sail on the water, they sail through it, with most of their bulk under the water interacting with the sea state.

If the ship is involved in action, thorough research as to positioning and damage needs to be employed in order to fix the action at a precise time. For many years I painted dust jackets for such authors as Dudley Pope and Patrick O'Brian. Clambering up the painted rigging, unfurling the watercolour sails and sailing on the acrylic sea, I always found the battle scenes vivid and dramatic in this 'wooden wall' period where the ships had to rapidly close each other before coming together like boxers in a clinch.

However, with action between steel warships, the protagonists are thousands of yards apart, one of the combatants is always a blob on the horizon, a thin trail of smoke marking its position and a tiny comma of flame showing the discharge of its guns. Thus, if you are painting 'steel', your subject is principally singular, framed by shell splashes and the flashes and smoke of its own guns. Yet the 'look' of a modern warship, even in harbour, suggests drama and sometimes menace.

Like the best cinema, movies that imply drama and menace are far more effective for not actually showing it. When you see an eighteenth century frigate under full sail it is a beautiful sight, full of wind and weather. When you show the battleship *Bismarck* under full power, the impression is of massive strength and implied menace.

ARCHITECTURE

Although steel warships followed the accepted practice of turrets fore and aft, with bridges, masts and funnels in between, there were a surprising number of architectural differences between the different nations. British warship designers favoured a perpendicular 'stately' appearance. During the inter-war period,

American battleships employed caged masts rather like upturned wicker baskets, whilst German warships stressed a massive built up appearance of bridges and funnels, with their heavy ships designed to a look-alike pattern. Italian warships seemed to have been designed by artists, whilst the most distinctive and unusual variations on this theme came from the famous Japanese designers Hiraga and Fujimoto, whose heavily-armed creations featured massive 'Pagoda' styled bridges, serpentine funnels and undulating decks quite unlike anything else afloat.

Today, the maritime painter has a more difficult task trying to make some kind of visual sense out of 'stealth' warships which appear to have been built to an international, homogenised and somewhat bland set of plans. Devoid of visibly proper masts, yards, radar arrays, guns and boats, the artist who paints steel warships must retreat into the past where dramatic, powerful and fabulous looking ships still exist and will sail the seas forever.

In 1986 I visited Portsmouth Naval Dockyard again, on the occasion of the visit by the battleship U.S.S *Iowa*, and like all 'geeks' I thought I would have the ship to myself for that day. The queue of the 'geek' army stretched from the railway station to the dockyard and would have raised the spirits of an A–list pop star; and they were all there for a fifty-year-old battleship. Although the age of the dreadnought battleship is well and truly over, the collective memory and awe that these great ships still inspire remains and will endure. As for me, a forty-year-old standing on the deck of the last U.S. battleship, I remembered the ten-year-old boy standing on the deck of the last British one as the might of Britain's naval supremacy slipped quietly away into the past.

H.M.S. *GIBRALTAR* 1896 British Armoured Cruiser

Sister ships: *Edgar, Endymion, Grafton, Hawke, Theseus*

Displacement	7,760 tons
Length	386 ft
Speed	20 Knots
Complement	544
Guns	2 - 9.2". 10 - 6"
Torpedo tubes	4 - 14"
Armour	6" Hull Belt

H.M.S. *Gibraltar* and her sisters were the oldest British cruisers to see service in World War One. In fact they were already nearly twenty years old when recalled to the colours, and this says something for their quality and sturdiness. Like all Royal Navy ships, especially cruisers, they were designed for world-wide service. Speedy, powerful and habitable they were convincing counters to French cruisers of the same period. They formed part of the 'Special Flying Squadron', a fleet that had to be ready to provision, raise steam and depart for any trouble spot throughout the world at a moment's notice. To this end each ship's supplies were kept permanently at their berths; powder and ammunition quite literally had their name on it, their machinery was kept at full readiness and their crews on full alert. Within a few days the Flying Squadron had to be at sea in the service of gunboat diplomacy. When the German Kaiser pledged support to the Boer President, Kruger, the 'Flying Squadron' was dispatched to the South African coast to prevent support for the Boers coming from the German navy.

An unusual feature of *Gibraltar* and some of her sisters was that their hulls were sheathed with copper and wood to protect them from marine growth in the tropics so that they could maintain a high turn of speed. This measure gave these ships added strength and stability in all weathers.

As pictured in this painting, H.M.S. *Gibraltar* is in full Victorian naval livery, as if on parade for the Queen herself. Shortly after the death of Queen Victoria, the Royal Navy adopted 'Battleship Grey' for all their vessels, an early attempt at 'stealth' technology as this colour actually absorbs colours, allowing for a measure of camouflage. The carnival confidence of the Victorian age had given way to the doubts and uncertainties of the twentieth century.

H.M.S. *Gibraltar*, oil on board, 24 x 32 inches

BRUIX 1894 French Armoured Cruiser

Sister ships: *Admiral Charmer, Chanzy, Latouche–Treville.*

Displacement	4681 tons
Speed	19 knots
Complement	393
Guns	2 - 7.6", 6 - 5.5"
Torpedo Tubes	4 -18"

Following the policy of torpedo-boats-or-bust advocated by the 'Jeunne Ecole' group of French naval theorists, wiser councils prevailed in the early 1890s and the navy of France returned to a mixed balanced force, with cruisers playing a leading role.

French cruisers were 'multi function' ships, serving the battlefleet as scouts, acting as commerce raiders and servicing the French overseas possessions as colonial cruisers.

The lead French ship of her day was the armoured cruiser *Dupy du Lome*. Fast and powerful, this ship was studied closely by foreign navies and influenced their building programmes. Following this revolutionary ship, four smaller cruisers were built to the same pattern. *Bruix* was a small armoured cruiser which packed a powerful punch. All the main guns were enclosed in turrets and could out-range those of most opposing ships in the same class. One of the most distinctive features of this ship was the extraordinary 'spoon bill' bow which seemed to hark back to the days of Grecian galleys. Whether this was meant to serve as a ram is in some doubt but this feature, and the somewhat top-heavy appearance of French warships of this period, tended to lead to instability and poor handling.

During World War One, two of these cruisers were sunk and one seriously damaged but *Bruix* led a charmed life, serving in the Red Sea, and helping to enforce an allied blockade of Greece when that country seemed to be falling into a German alliance. She was eventually broken up in 1920.

Bruix, oil on canvas, 20 x 24 inches

JAUREGUIBERRY 1897 French Battleship

Displacement	11,637 tons
Length	356 ft
Speed	17.6 knots
Complement	631
Guns	2 - 12", 2 -10.8", 8 - 5.5"
Armour	17" hull belt, Turrets 15"

Following the Franco–Prussian war, the French navy fell under the influence of a group of naval theorists called the 'Jeunne Ecole' who argued that as the French could not out-build their main rival, the British, they should adopt the new naval weapons, the torpedo and the torpedo boat at the expense of battleships and heavy cruisers. They envisioned swarms of torpedo boats falling upon helpless battleships, destroying them and Britain's naval advantage. However, the holes in this strategy were obvious: the limited fighting power and technology of torpedo boats and the ability of battleships to defend themselves with a hurricane of shellfire forced the French to rethink their naval building programmes and battleship and cruisers eventually won the day.

However, owing to the unstable political climate in France in the 1890s, major warship construction was an inordinately time-consuming process and *Jaureguiberry* took nearly seven years to build and was thus all but obsolete at the time of her commissioning in 1897.

Allied to this, warship design in France was plagued with differing ideas and theories so each major warship was virtually a 'one-off', in fact the French navy was called 'The Fleet of Samples' by their rivals. Thus *Jaureguiberry* was singular in many respects but she did introduce several novel features including electrically operated gun turrets and a powerful armament on a limited displacement. Unfortunately, this also meant a shortened hull and heavy upperworks which limited speed and made the ship somewhat unsteady.

Additionally, French warships of this period were built with a pronounced 'tumblehome' to the hull form which meant that the beam of the ships was considerably wider at the waterline than across the decks. Part of this was to enable the wing turrets a wider field of fire but this feature led to further instability, and gave the ships a strangely old-fashioned appearance, rather like the wooden walls of Nelson's time.

Although well past her best by 1914, *Jaureguiberry* was pressed into service at the outbreak of the Great War as a convoy escort in the Mediterranean, shelling the Turkish forts in the Dardanelles and providing sterling work in her country's war effort. *Jaureguiberry* finally ended her long life in the scrapyard at Toulon in 1934.

Jaureguiberry, oil on paper, 18 x 25 inches

H.M.S. *LONDON*   1902   British Battleship

Sister ships: *Bulwark, Venerable, Queen, Prince of Wales.*

Displacement	15,000 tons
Length	430 ft
Speed	19 knots
Complement	810
Guns	4 - 12", 12 - 6", 16 - 16pdrs
Torpedoes	4 - 18" tubes
Armour	12" belt, 10" turrets

H.M.S. *London* was among the largest class of battleship built for the Royal Navy. They were part a standardised design of battleships by the Chief of Naval Construction, Sir William White, in the late Victorian era. With the early 'Majestic' design, the funnels were mounted side-by-side but the bulk of the class had their funnels in the usual tandem pattern, otherwise this clever design allowed for continuous improvement and upgrading when new advances in armament, armour and engineering came on stream.

In all 37 battleships of this basic design were commissioned into the Royal Navy, but with the coming of H.M.S. *Dreadnought* in 1906, with her all big gun design and her high speed turbine propulsion, all of Sir william White's pre-dreadnought battleships were rendered obsolete at a stroke. This large class of warship never found itself in the line of battle with the Grand Fleet but were used in the dangerous waters around the Dardanelles where three of them were lost to torpedoes and mines. However, H.M.S. *London* survived to be reconstructed as a large mine layer carrying 240 mines. She was finally scrapped in 1920.

In 1912 when the ten-year-old battleship was beginning to show her age, H.M.S. *London* participated in an experiment into the future of naval warfare, the launching whilst the ship was underway, of a rickety biplane from a ramp over the forward part of the ship. Nobody who took part in these experiments could have known that this tiny, flimsy aircraft would be the harbinger of the mighty aerial armadas that would, within 25 years, wrest control of the seas and doom the battleship forever.

H.M.S. *London* taking on stores, acrylic on paper, 16.5 x 24 inches

THE BATTLE OF TSUSHIMA 27 May 1905

At the turn of the twentieth century Russia should have been the greatest and most important power on earth. With huge deposits of mineral wealth, an almost limitless land mass and an equally limitless population, her military power should have been enough to deter any potential rival. In practice, the Russian state was wedded to an almost feudal social structure with a top heavy monarchy and a teeming mass of illiterate workers and peasants who had only just been released from serfdom. This grossly unequal society was riven by class conflict and corruption and ruled over by an astonishingly weak and vacillating ruler, Tsar Nicholas II. Any form of advancement in his country was predicated on whom you knew, whose arm you had to twist and how clever you were in playing the game of court intrigue. Russia's nearest rival on the Pacific rim was Japan, a country with a history and traditions even older than Russia's but also a country wholeheartedly modernising its social structure and its military in rapid order so as to establish its place in the world.

With the conclusion of her successful war with China in 1895, the emerging Japan sought to legitimise her conquests of Port Arthur and the Liao-Ting peninsula with the international community. However France, Germany and especially Russia, fearing the emerging power of Japan, forced a peace treaty on her which required her to give up her Chinese conquests in return for absorbing Korea into the Japanese Empire. Shortly after this, in an extraordinary act of bad faith and duplicity, Russia forced the weakened Chinese to lease to them the base of Port Arthur and to allow them to build a railway to it through Manchuria. To the Japanese, this action could not be allowed to go unpunished so she bided her time and quietly built up her army and navy to a level that would enable her to strike the Russians down.

The Japanese navy was trained and equipped by the British. Her traditions were modelled on those of the Royal Navy and the Samurai warrior caste. Japanese naval officers and men were rewarded and promoted through merit alone and one of these emerged to rival the military feats of Horatio Nelson himself. Admiral Heimachoro Togo the commander of the Japanese Navy in 1905, was quiet, studious, phlegmatic and a master tactician. He had served some of his naval career in England, observed the Royal Navy at first hand and had made a study of British shipyards and the latest trends in naval technology and tactics

On a cold February night in 1904 he raised this signal in homage to his hero Nelson, "Our enemy flies the Russian Flag, the fate of the Empire depends on our success, let every man do his utmost." Then, without a declaration of war, he sent his torpedo boats to attack the unsuspecting Russians at anchor in their base at Port Arthur. Although this attack was not as damaging as Togo had hoped, from this point on any luck in war that the Russians may have enjoyed completely deserted them. Within months their best admiral, Makaroff, had run into a Russian minefield, his flagship had blown up with the admiral killed. His competent successor Witjeff offered battle to the Japanese but was hit by a shell and no trace of his remains was ever found. All this time the Russian Far East fleet was trapped in Port Arthur surrounded by Japanese guns which slowly and deliberately destroyed it in detail.

By now the Russian government was desperate to salvage some honour from a disastrous campaign. A new battlefleet was created from the modern battleships of the Baltic fleet plus some very ancient tonnage cobbled together from every corner of the Russian Empire. Its mission was to destroy Togo and to raise the siege of Port Arthur. To command this fleet Tsar Nicholas chose Admiral Rojdestvensky, a hard working but somewhat unstable officer prone to almost wild fits of temper and moods of dark depression. He set sail in October 1904 with his sovereign's good will and very little hope of success. Almost as soon as he had raised anchor, Rojdestvensky's flagship Suvaroff ran aground, then on passage through the North Sea he had attacked a fleet of British trawlers thinking they were Japanese torpedo boats resulting in being chased out of northern waters by the Royal Navy. The Russians struggled on through numerous breakdowns and near mutinies before rounding the Horn and reaching Madagascar where Rojdestvensky suffered a nervous breakdown. After a protracted stay on the island the Russian Fleet was assembled, with more ancient craft joining them before they set sail for the South China Sea, the straits of Tsushima and Admiral Togo.

The bad news continued to get worse for the Russians. Rojdestvenky's second in command was making the final leg of his journey dead in his coffin aboard his ship and the Commander refused to inform the rest of his ships for fear of lowering morale even further.

Then came the news that Port Arthur had fallen to the Japanese. The epic journey, one of the most extraordinary in maritime history had all been for nothing. All the fleet could do was to try and make their way to Vladivostok on Russia's Pacific coast. And Togo was still waiting.

As the Russian fleet groped its way through the straits of Tsushima in a protective fog their hopes began to rise a little, perhaps they might be able to pass through unobserved, perhaps they might just make it. Then the fog cleared revealing Admiral Togo's full battle line in perfect formation ready to do battle. The Russians opened fire first almost as if to relieve the tension.

Illustration for a bookjacket for *The Floating Madhouse* (Little Brown), acrylic on paper 15 x 22 inches

Togo carefully placed his ships in the most advantageous position before opening a murderous hurricane of accurate fire disabling the Russian flagship, *Suvaroff* and forcing her to pull out of line, thus throwing the remainder of the following ships into total confusion. The next ship, the battleship *Oslyabya* had the whole of her armour plating blown off one side and she sank like a stone, and the next battleship blew up. The carnage went on and on all day, and through the night with relentless torpedo boat attacks and into the next morning. Finally the few ships left surrendered, only two escaping out of a fleet of some forty vessels. It is probably the most complete and annihilating naval victory in all history, perhaps even greater than Trafalgar for whilst Napoleon still survived to rage across Europe and the Iberian peninsula, the Battle of Tsushima destroyed the Russian power in the Far East for forty years and ushered in a prominent new power in the Pacific region, creating a completely new naval tradition for the Japanese overnight

The thoroughly beaten Russians both on land and sea, suffered a revolution which was crushed only to suffer another and final revolution in 1917 which destroyed the Tsar, his family and the entire Court . But the seeds of this revolution were sown in the seas off Japan on a cold wet day in May 1905.

S.M.S. *SCHARNHORST* 1907 German Armoured Cruiser

Sister ship: *Gneisenau*

Displacement	(full load) 12,781 tons
Length	474.7 ft (144.6 m)
Beam	71 ft (21.6 m)
Speed	22.7 knots
Complement	764
Guns	8 - 8. 2", 6 - 5.9", 18 - 3.45"
Torpedo tubes	4
Armour	Hull belt 6" Deck 2"

S.M.S. *Scharnhorst* and her sister ship *Gneisenau* represented the high point of armoured (heavy) cruiser construction in Germany prior to World War One. In fact so well balanced was she in terms of firepower, armour and endurance that *Scharnhorst* was one of the classic ships of her kind ever built. She and her sister were designed for endurance as she was slated to be the flagship of the German East Asia Squadron protecting German colonies and interests in the Far East and the Pacific ocean. These colonies consisted of the Marianas, the Caroline and the Marshall Islands and further south the Bismarck archipelago, the Solomon Islands, German New Guinea and New Mecklenburg. The East Asia Squadron was based in the leased German port of Tsingtao on the coast of China. This little piece of Germany in the Far East boasted a well stocked German library, a grammar school to teach Chinese children German, two busy hotels and a famous brewery, Tsingtao beer is still produced and enjoyed today.

The *Scharnhorst* and *Gneisenau* were the crack gunnery ships in the Kaiser's navy and it was fitting that the new commander of the East Asia Squadron was one of the German navy's best gunnery experts. Vice Admiral Graf von Spee, a courteous, resolute and patient man, looked every inch the aristocrat he was and was much admired within the fleet. Perhaps his only vice was he was addicted to the game of bridge and this gambling part of his nature would bring him both glory and eventually disaster. Throughout the summer of 1914 an air of expectation and concern hung over the German colonies in China and the Pacific. The endless round of social duties and entertaining foreign warships centred upon von Spee and his ships. These duties included a visit to Hong Kong as the guests of H.M.S. *Monmouth*, a ship they would meet again under very different circumstances. Von Spee realised that should war break out in Europe, Britain would call upon her ally Japan to help protect British interests in the Far East. The Japanese fleet was the most formidable in the Pacific, and the German colonies including Tsingtao would quickly fall prey to the ambitious Japanese. As the German ships left Tsingtao for a visit to the South Pacific possession on the 20 June, many in the fleet must have wondered if they would ever see the little colony again.

S.M.S. *Scharnhorst*, acrylic on paper, 14 x 18 inches

S.M.S. *SCHARNHORST* 2

As the German East Asia squadron headed by its flagship., the armoured cruiser *Scharnhorst* arrived in the Mariana Islands, the first reports of the assassination of the Austrian Archduke Franz Ferdinand in Sarajevo reached them. When vice Admiral Graf von Spee moved on to the Caroline Islands he received a telegraph from Berlin warning him that "The political situation is not entirely satisfactory". As he sailed further east to the island of Panope, von Spee ordered the light cruiser *Nurnberg* sailing west to China to divert and join him. As well as this, the cruiser *Emden* was also ordered to Panope from Tsingtao. When they arrived the East Asia squadron consisted of the armoured cruisers *Scharnhorst* and *Gneisenau* and the light cruisers *Leipzig, Dresden, Emden* and *Nurnburg* with assorted colliers and support ships. As these warships gathered a message was received from the Kaiser himself which read "From the moment war breaks out, each captain must make his own decisions. Above all the officer must bear in mind that his chief duty is to damage the enemy as severely as

possible. If he succeeds in winning an honourable place for his ships in the history of the German navy, I will assure him of my Imperial favour." In spite of the rather overblown rhetoric, the Kaiser's message was clear: "It's up to you, what ever you do, do it gloriously!"

To a man of von Spee's bearing and sense of duty, the import of the Kaiser's instructions was clear, to fight his way back to Germany wreaking destruction along the way should war be declared.

His ships were ready, but which way to go? The way west was barred by the Japanese, the way south towards Australia would possibly lead to an engagement with the fast, powerful battlecruiser H.M.A.S *Australia*, more than a match for any of his ships. The only realistic option was the west coast of Chile which was friendly towards Germany.. Before this, he released the *Emden* to conduct a raiding campaign in the Indian Ocean. As the expected war broke out, the East Asia Squadron set course eastward across the Pacific.

Admiral von Spee Crosses the Atlantic, oil on canvas, 28 x 30 inches

H.M.S. *GOOD HOPE* 1902 British Armoured Cruiser

Displacement	14,100 tons
Length	535 ft
Beam	71 ft
speed	24 knots
Guns	2 - 9.2, 16 - 6"
Torpedo tubes	2
Armour	Hull belt 6"
Deck	2 - 3"
Complement	900

When H.M.S. *Good Hope* was built in 1902 she was, on paper, a fast, powerful and capable armoured cruiser, a match for anything of her kind in the world. By 1914 she was old, worn out and woefully undergunned. Even the layout of what guns she carried left a lot to be desired with one 9.2" slow-firing cannon at each end of the ship and her 6" guns buried in casemates strung along the length of the hull placing them too close to the waterline making them difficult to aim and keep dry in any sort of sea. When the war broke out she was languishing in semi retirement at Portsmouth. Recommissioned in some haste, she was given a scratch crew of naval reservists who had to learn how to handle their ship on their way down to the West Indies. Yet H.M.S. *Good Hope* was to be the flagship of Cradock's South Atlantic Squadron. Rear Admiral Sir Christopher Cradock was an officer totally devoted to the Royal Navy and its service since he joined at the age of 13. With no family of his own, the navy was his whole life, its traditions his bible. Much admired in the Fleet and decorated as a fearless leader, he certainly deserved a better hand of cards than that dealt by fate and the Admiralty. As it was, with a collection of elderly ships and inexperienced crews, he was tasked with intercepting the powerful German squadron proceeding towards South America.

Sailing down the east coast of South America, Cradock was bombarded by a blizzard of orders and instructions from the Admiralty, some of them misleading and contradictory but all amounting to one thing, seek out the German East Asia Squadron and destroy it. Winston Churchill, the first Lord of the Admiralty, promised the hapless Cradock all manner of powerful ships and support including H.M.S. *Defence* one of the latest armoured cruisers and more than a match for any one of von Spee's ships. However the closer

Cradock got to the Falkland Islands, the more hollow these promises became. In the end all he got was an ancient battleship, H.M.S. *Canopus*, a ship so slow that she could barely get out of her own way. However the First Lord grandly described this museum piece as "A citadel around which our cruisers in these waters could find absolute security." This was typical Churchillian rhetoric reflecting his passion for micromanaging the Admiralty and the movements of its ships with confusing and often contradictory instructions.

By the time Cradock reached the Falklands his actual squadron consisted of *Good Hope, Monmouth*, the light cruiser *Glasgow* and the armed liner *Otranto*. Later H.M.S. *Canopus* steamed slowly into port with her motley crew of elderly reservists, coast guard veterans and boy sailors, and a chief engineer who had locked himself in his cabin and gone quietly insane. These were the only reinforcements that Cradock would receive and so it was little wonder that he began to view his mission with a certain degree of fatalism. Writing to a friend before his fateful voyage, Cradock made the revealing comment which goes some way to explain his subsequent actions: "At least I will take care not to suffer the fate of poor Troubridge". In August 1914, Admiral Troubridge had avoided battle in the Mediterranean against the German battlecruiser *Goeben* believing he was carrying out Admiralty orders not to engage a superior enemy. As this ran contrary to the Nelsionic motto "Engage the enemy more closely" and his actions resulted in the *Goeben* gifting herself to Turkey which in turn, turned that country into Germany's ally, Troubrige was recalled to Britain in disgrace, his career in ruins. This was not to be the fate of Rear Admiral Sir Christopher Cradock. According to one of his captains, as the brave Cradock set course for the coast of Chile, he already knew that he was sailing to his doom.

H.M.S. *Good Hope* and H.M.S. *Monmouth* depart the Falkland Islands, watercolour on paper, 14 x 21 inches

H.M.S. *GOOD HOPE* 2

As Sir Christopher Craddock's small fleet of cruisers and support ships rounded the straits of Magellan, he had dispatched H.M.S. *Glasgow* to the Chilean port of Coronel to scout out possible sightings of von Spee and to collect messages from the British Consulate. When the *Glasgow* arrived there it began to pick up German wireless traffic from the light cruiser *Leipzig*. Thus informed, Cradock set course for Coronel to intercept this lone German ship. As he approached, the enemy radio signals suddenly became more intense. It was obvious that many more German ships were in the area and that battle would soon be joined. As *Glasgow* rejoined the *Good Hope*, smoke on the horizon announced the arrival of the entire German squadron. As both fleets literally sailed into battle, Cradock left the *Canopus* in the rear and positioned himself west of the Germans with the setting sun at his back so as to dazzle the German gun layers.

The patient von Spee held his fire until the sun had dipped below the horizon thus enabling his ships to merge into the landscape to the east whilst the British ships were vividly outlined against the afterglow. At 7.04, with the wind rising, *Canopus* received one last characteristic message from Cradock – "I am going to attack the enemy now".

At that moment, von Spee opened fire.

Against the setting sun, HMS *Good Hope* turns to face the German East Asia Squadron off the coast of Coronel. (*Collection of Dan S. Somekh*)

The first salvo the *Scharnhorst* fired at the *Good Hope* fell short, the second over, whilst the third smashed into the forward turret setting the forepart of the ship ablaze. At a stroke Cradock's flagship's power had been reduced by half. Whilst the *Gneisenau* concentrated on the *Monmouth* and the Leipzig tackled the *Glasgow*, Cradock realised that if he stood any chance of bringing his 6" batteries into range he would have to close with the enemy, but the Germans backed away, all the while maintaining a fabulously accurate rate of fire. In spite of suffering murderous damage to his ships, Cradock kept coming on. Soon his ships were ablaze from stem to stern but still he tried to close with the Germans. With *Good Hope*'s bridge shot away and his masts and funnels collapsing around him, Cradock never gave up but charged directly at the *Scharnhorst*.

Von Spee and his sailors were lost in admiration at the tenacity of their enemy but they had a job to do and soon the *Good Hope* was smothered with devastating shell fire culminating in a blinding flash as the forward magazine exploded blowing the ship in half. As the rest of wreck drifted away still firing her 6" guns, a last act of defiance, the *Good Hope* disappeared into history, only her dead drifting on the rising waves marked her passing.

With the destruction of the *Monmouth* and the flight of the *Glasgow* and *Otranto*, the terrible Battle of Coronel was over. None of the German ships were damaged to any great extent and none of their crews were injured. Of the *Good Hope* and *Monmouth*, no one survived. They did not sell their lives dearly, they were annihilated.

Much debate and speculation still surrounds the Battle of Coronel, the worst defeat up to that time inflicted on the Royal Navy since the eighteenth century. Should Sir Christopher Cradock have fallen back on the *Canopus* and shadowed von Spee until adequate reinforcements arrived? With the benefit of hindsight this probably would have been the wisest course, but this fails to take into account the nature of Cradock and the shadow of the Troubridge debacle hanging over him and the navy. Taking all these things into consideration it is impossible to imagine that he could have acted in any other way other than the way he did. However a good measure of blame must attach itself to Winston Churchill, his Chief of Staff Admiral Sir Doveton Sturdee and the Admiralty. It was they who failed to appreciate the danger they were putting Cradock into with his inadequate force and it was they who failed to provide him with the reinforcements and support necessary for him to accomplish his task. At best what support they offered was half-hearted and at worst it amounted to criminal negligence.

As a result, 1,600 good men and their brave admiral died needlessly on that terrible late afternoon off the coast of Chile on 1 November, 1914.

H.M.S. *Good Hope* and H.M.S. *Monmouth* are destroyed at Coronel, acrylic on paper, 14.5 x 18.5 inches (bookjacket: *Buller's Victory* Richard Hough, Transworld)

H.M.S. CANOPUS 1897 British Battleship

Sister ships: *Albion, Glory, Goliath, Ocean, Vengeance*

Displacement	13,360 (Full load) tons
Length	421.6 ft (128.47m)
Guns	4 - 12", 12 - 6", 10 - 12"
Torpedo tubes	4
Armour	6" hull belt, 8" turrets
Speed	18 knots
Crew	682

Most designers of warships are fairly anonymous figures, their creations taking on a life of their own once commissioned whilst their designers remain in the shadows of the civil service. Even the epoch-making H.M.S. *Dreadnought* was designed by a committee lead by Admiral Sir John Fisher, the First Sea Lord and Sir Philip Watts the Director of Naval Construction. However, the designer of H.M.S. *Canopus* and her sisters, Sir William White, was very much a public figure, the brains behind the power of the late Victorian battlefield. In office from 1886 to 1903 White created the classic British pre-*Dreadnought* battleship design, heavy guns fore and aft, secondary armament spread amidships with two equally-spaced funnels gracing a stately looking vessel.

For the first time in the Royal Navy, White's ships were built to a recognisable pattern which when perfected, endured up until the coming of the *Dreadnought* in 1906. The *Canopus* introduced many novel features in her day including small tube boilers for more efficient steaming, Krupp cemented armour plate which was stronger and lighter than conventional armour and guns that could be loaded at any elevation allowing for more rapid fire. All of this was fairly groundbreaking in 1897 but 9 years later, H.M.S. *Dreadnought* with her massively increased firepower and high speed turbines were to render all contemporary battleships obsolete at a stroke. Sir William White, whose illustrious career was founded upon these earlier ships fell from favour when the Royal Yacht he designed had capsized in dry dock, was retired in some disgrace and spent the rest of his life writing critical letters against the new warship revolution.

Like their designer, the *Canopus* and her sisters were progressively reduced to second class status within the navy, serving out their useful lives in far flung foreign stations and it was in this capacity that *Canopus* was dispatched as a reinforcement to Admiral Sir Christopher Cradock's fleet of equally elderly cruisers in their hunt for Admiral Graf von Spee's crack Pacific squadron in the southern oceans. When she arrived in Port Stanley, it was found that she could only make 12 knots at best maximum speed, her engines had all but broken down and so had her chief engineer who had to be secured in his cabin under a suicide watch. Although the Admiralty's orders were for Cradock to meet von Spee in concert with the *Canopus*, her wretched condition forced him to leave her in the rear, protecting his colliers whilst he forged on ahead to search for the German ships. When H.M.S. *Glasgow* rejoined the *Canopus* after the Coronel disaster both ships and their colliers beat a retreat to the Falkland Islands to await further instructions from London.

In Port Stanley harbour, the *Canopus* was run aground on a sand bank to act as a guardship should von Spee decide to attack the Falklands. The day after Admiral Sturdee and his battlecruisers arrived at this distant outpost, so did von Spee. The Battle of the Falkland Islands began with *Canopus* opening blind fire at the *Gneisenau* over the hill overlooking the harbour and almost hitting her. As the German cruiser retreated and Sturdee's battlefleet had set sail to follow her, H.M.S. *Canopus'* great moment in history had passed.

Following the action off the Falklands, *Canopus* was sent to lend fire support to the Dardanelles landings but survived to make it back to the UK where she spent the rest of her days in honourable retirement as an accommodation ship in Chatham.

H.M.S. *Canopus* was much admired in her heyday as the classic example of the British pre-*Dreadnought* ship of the line. However, history will always remember her as the old, slow and inadequate reinforcement to a British commander in a desperate situation, far away from home. This is perhaps the unfair but inevitable consequence in the life of a once-major warship, whose useful life was long past when the trumpets of battle sounded.

H.M.S. Canopus, acrylic on paper, 16 x 24 inches

H.M.S. *INVINCIBLE* 1908 British Battlecruiser

Sister ships: *Inflexible Indomitable*

Displacement	(full load) 20,135 tons
Length	567 ft (172.8 m)
Beam	78.5 ft (23.9m)
Speed	25 Knots
Complement	784
Guns	8 - 12", 12 - 4"
Torpedo Tubes	5
Armour	Hull belt 6"
Decks	2.5"
Turrets	7"

H.M.S. *Invincible* was a new class of warship, so new and revolutionary that a whole new category had to be invented to describe her. Originally classed as armoured cruisers, they and their like became 'battlecruisers'. Such a name carried a ring of power and speed and not a little glamour, however this proved to be a dangerous misnomer as it tempted admirals and captains to put such ships in the battle line. Conceived by Sir John Fisher of *Dreadnought* fame, he saw such a ship as so powerful and fast as to be able to catch any enemy cruiser, yet to be able to outpace a well-armoured battleship.

The battlecruiser's other function was to act as a fast scout for the battlefleet, destroying enemy cruisers and destroyers, operating on the edge of the main fleet action itself. Like the Japanese super battleships thirty years later, a certain amount of secrecy and deceit attended their published specifications in order to fool the Germans. The ruse worked to perfection as the German reply was the *Blücher*, an armoured cruiser with 8.2" guns and triple expansion engines. When built, *Invincible* and her sisters carried 12" battleship guns and were powered by the latest turbines. The *Blücher* was completely outclassed . As the *Invincible* rendered all armoured cruisers obsolete at a stroke on their completion, they were the only show in town. However this held only as long as competitor nations didn't build any battlecruisers of their own and three years later the Germans did just that when they commissioned the *Von Der Tann*. A battlecruiser race had

started and it was this race that the Germans with the quality of their ships, ultimately won.

The departure of the first sea lord, Lord Louis Battenburg, a victim of anti-German hysteria and a scullerous press campaign, bought Sir John Fisher back to the Admiralty as its naval head. His reappointment coincided with the news of the Coronel disaster and although Fisher was in his seventies, this event was to show that the old admiral had lost none of his drive and determination. He immediately ordered *Invincible* and *Inflexible* south from Scotland to Devonport to take on ammunition and stores along with Churchill's newly-appointed commander of the South Atlantic, the chief of staff at the Admiralty, Sir Frederick Doveton Sturdee. Churchill's choice of Admiral Sturdee was a shrewd one. Sturdee was a cool and calculating tactician, brave under fire and without the impetuosity of Cradock. It also suited Fisher whose dislike of Sturdee was well known. Sturdee's brief was to hasten down to the Falkland Islands to await the expected arrival of von Spee. Fisher calculated that if Sturdee failed in his mission then Sturdee would be blamed for everything, however, if the mission succeeded, Fisher would take all the glory. The loss of Cradock and all his men was a tragedy and a public relations disaster of the first magnitude, for the sake of the Royal Navy the slate had to be wiped clean.

Admiral von Spee not only had to be defeated, he had to be crushed.

H.M.S. *Invincible*, acrylic on paper, 17 x 25 inches

Following the Battle of Coronel, von Spee's exploits were fêted all over Germany. His victory was a terrific tonic for the new German navy, they had taken on ships of the greatest naval power and won. However the sinking of two elderly cruisers was not the defeat of the Royal Navy and von Spee knew it. He had expended nearly half his ammunition in the recent battle, he lacked a reliable support system and coaling stations and was thousands of miles from Germany. Added to this he was facing an implacable enemy determined to hunt him down. The obvious course of action would be to disappear into the broad Atlantic and make for Germany, coaling from German ships out of New York and at the Azores if the Portuguese were still friendly to Germany. But von Spee had other plans, he would attack the Falkland Islands, take what coal he needed and burning the rest whilst also destroying the important wireless station.

Most of his captains agreed with their admiral's plan. One who did not was Captain Julius Maerker of the *Gneisenau*, Spee's closest confident and friend who felt the plan too risky and would give away their position when secrecy on the passage to Germany was paramount But the gambler in von Spee's makeup overruled his friend's caution and as the fleet made passage around the Horn, he dispatched the *Gneisenau* and *Nurnberg* to scout out and attack the Falklands.

As 8 December dawned clear and bright the lookout on the hill overlooking Port Stanley spotted smoke on the horizon. Below him, hidden from the sea, lay the purposely grounded *Canopus* with her guns ready and beyond her the fleet that had arrived the previous evening comprising *Invincible* and *Inflexible* and the light cruisers *Kent, Carnarvon, Bristol, Cornwall,* and the survivor of Coronel, *Glasgow*. All the ships were completing coaling when Sturdee received the news of the German approach and as he calmly called for steam to be raised he ordered his men to breakfast.

When the *Gneisenau* was in range, *Canopus* opened fire, her shells nearly hitting the German ship. Then the Germans spotted the tripod masts behind the low hills which only meant one thing - battlecruisers. Radioing a warning to von Spee, Maerker beat a hasty retreat. The chase was on.

There could never have been any doubt as to the outcome of the coming battle, Sturdee had the whole day to catch his quarry, the visibility was perfect and he could control the range and the battle. As the *Invincible* and *Inflexible* gained on von Spee the German admiral released his lighter ships to the south whilst he and the *Gneisenau* turned north to face the British. Sturdee had anticipated this move and in turn released his lighter ships to the chase south whilst he opened fire on the *Scharnhorst,* and *Inflexible* on the *Gneisenau*. The Battle of the Falkland Islands had begun.

The major part of the action lasted some three hours, the Germans proving again and again why they were the crack gunnery ships of the fleet. The *Invincible* was hit at least 36 times but received no appreciable damage.

After a slow start and hampered to start with by each others' smoke the British ships began to destroy the German ships in detail. *Scharnhorst,* absolutely wrecked, fought to the last man before capsizing with all her surviving crew, including von Spee himself. *Gneisenau* took longer to succumb but finally, riddled with shot and shell, she scuttled herself. Over a hundred men were rescued but not Heinrich von Spee, the Admiral's son. His other son was lost when the *Nurnberg* and *Leipzig* were sunk far to the south. Only the *Dresden* escaped to be finally cornered and scuttled a few weeks later.

The German East Asia Squadron was utterly destroyed and Fisher's battlecruiser concept had been gloriously vindicated. Even the *Emden* was lost to the guns of H.M.A.S *Sydney* in the Indian Ocean after a short, successful raiding career. Thus the last German ships in the southern oceans disappeared. From now on the naval war would shift to the north Atlantic, the North Sea and the Mediterranean. The gallant Maximillian Graf von Spee and his men had fought to the last in proud tradition of the German Navy. For this they paid a terrible price but the essential humility of their admiral was reflected in his last signal to his friend Captain Maerker who had opposed the Falklands operation "You were right after all".

After releasing his lighter warships, Admiral von Spee turns to port to engage the British forces off the Falkland Islands. (*Collection of Dan S. Somekh*)

S.M.S. *SEYDLITZ* 1913 German Battlecruiser

Displacement	24,610 tons
Length	658 ft
Armour	11.8" hull belt, 8" turrets.
Speed	26 knots
Complement	1,068
Guns	10 - 11", 12 - 5.9", 14 -3.5"
Torpedoes	4 - 19.7"

General Friedrich Wilhelm Freiherr von Seydlitz was a dashing cavalry officer in the service of the Prussian King, Frederick the Great. Seydlitz had great personal courage and this spirit was certainly the hallmark of the famous German battlecruiser named after him.

The fourth ship of this type to be commissioned into the Kaiser's navy, she followed the construction principles of her predecessors, great strength, complex watertight subdivision and high speed, *Seydlitz* also had a high focs'le to aid stability and seaworthiness. German ships were noted for their ability to withstand heavy punishment and still remain dangerous opponents. *Seydlitz* was a well-loved ship by all her crew including her long-serving captain Moritz von Egidy who saw her through all her major battles, and by his wife who always awaited 'her' ship when it came into port and shouted instructions to her husband on his bridge as to how to berth 'their' beloved battlecruiser.

However, this beautiful ship was also a man-of-war and the fleet flagship of Admiral Franz von Hipper the commander of the German battlecruiser squadron. Throughout the latter part of 1914 and early 1915, Hipper conducted 'tip and run' raids on the east coast towns of Yarmouth, Lowestoft, Hartlepool, Whitby and Scarborough in order to tempt the light cruiser forces to come out to do battle. But on 24 January 1915, this resulted in a meeting between the Germans and the British battlecruisers of Admiral Beatty.

The Battle of Dogger Bank was a tremendous running fight across the north sea and 30 minutes into this battle *Seydlitz* received a shell into the rearmost turret which exploded into flame. As the panic-stricken turret crew sought escape into the next turret this too caught fire, the resulting inferno setting off 6000kg of powder; 165 men were incinerated in an instant. This terrible fire seemed set to destroy the ship so the chief gunnery officer, determined to sell her dearly, ordered rapid fire from the remaining turrets. As salvo after salvo thundered out a warrant officer and his heroic team managed to brave the fire and turn on the red hot valves which flooded the rear turret magazines and extinguished the fire, thus saving the ship.

The Battle of Dogger Bank was over and Hipper bought his battlecruisers home but he had lost the armoured cruiser *Blücher*. In the following year an even sterner test awaited *Seydlitz*. The Battle of Jutland was the greatest naval gun battle in recorded history involving the entire battlefleets of Germany and Britain and the battlecruisers were in the thick of it from first to last. Hipper's flag was in the S.M.S. *Lutzow*, with *Seydlitz* third in the line. As the shells rained down up on the battlecruisers of Hipper and Beatty, *Seydlitz* and S.M.S. *Derflinger* found themselves opposing H.M.S. *Queen Mary*, Beatty's crack gunnery battlecruiser.

As *Queen Mary* began to hit *Seydlitz* the German ship, in concert with *Derflinger*, loosed off salvos which found their mark with deadly accuracy blowing the H.M.S. *Queen Mary* to pieces. At that moment Beatty saw the German High Seas Fleet and turned north to lead them on to the guns of the Grand Fleet. As the two fleets met gigantic battle was joined and *Seydlitz* was hit again and again, but she was still a very dangerous opponent and when the armoured cruiser H.M.S. *Defence* blundered across the German line, *Seydlitz* went for her, pouring devastating fire into the unfortunate British cruiser which eventually blew up with a shattering explosion. By the time the battle was broken off, *Seydlitz* had received 21 heavy shell hits and one torpedo. She had 98 men killed and 55 wounded, and with 5308 tons of water on board she was well down by the head and in a sinking condition. With brilliant seamanship, Captain von Egidy nursed the stricken battlecruiser home, terribly damaged but still afloat.

It became clear that with the terrible turret fires at Dogger Bank, *Seydlitz* had inadvertently saved many German ships at the Battle of Jutland. By the time this battle was joined the German navy had put many safety measures into their handling of ammunition and the results of Jutland told their own story. The British lost five heavy ships to magazine explosions whilst the Germans lost none to this cause.

After this, S.M.S. *Seydlitz* had one more sad duty to perform, on a cold foggy north sea day in 1918 she led the surrendered High Seas Fleet into captivity at Scapa Flow. Yet in spite of the occasion, no one could have denied that the place at the head of the German Fleet rightly belonged to *Seydlitz*, the bravest ship in the fleet and one of the greatest in the history of naval warfare.

S.M.S. *Seydlitz* at Anchor, acrylic on paper, 16 x 24 inches

THE BATTLE OF DOGGER BANK 24 January 1915

By early 1915 the Commander of the German battlecruisers, Rear Admiral Franz von Hipper, began to suspect that the Royal Navy had knowledge of the intended operations and movements of the German navy in advance of these operations. He became convinced that this information was being relayed to the British by the fishing trawlers working the Dogger Bank area of the North Sea so he drew up plans to destroy these trawler 'spies' once and for all. In fact Hipper was correct, the British did have foreknowledge of the German navy's operational plans but they were not getting this information from spy trawlers but from the German naval codes which had been obligingly passed to them by the Russians who had captured a grounded German cruiser in the Baltic. These precious codes were encrypted by Room 40, a secret code breaking department based in the Admiralty. This information was to prove invaluable to the British war effort. German naval signals were received and encoded before the Germans had even left port on their operations. Admirals Jellicoe and Beatty had priceless information as to the whereabouts of every German ship.

On 23 January 1915 Hipper set in his flagship *Seydlitz* with the other German battlecruisers, *Moltke, Derflinger* and the armoured cruiser *Blücher,* with light cruiser and destroyer support. As a result of Room 40's latest information concerning this operation, Beatty in the *Lion* with the battlecruisers *Princess Royal, Tiger, New Zealand* and *Indomitable* weighed anchor at the same time to meet the unsuspecting Hipper off the Dogger Bank. At 8am the next morning both fleets sighted each other with Hipper twelve miles ahead and making for home. However the German admiral was restricted by the speed of the slowest ship in his squadron *Blücher* at 23 knots. On the other hand Beatty could press on with his speed of 28 knots and he soon began to overhaul the fleeing Germans. As the faster British ships passed along the German line, the rear enemy ship, the slow *Blücher*, was shelled by each of Beatty's battlecruisers in turn and soon she was in trouble. As both fleets charged southwards, H.M.S. *Lion* began to score hits on Hipper's flagship *Seydlitz* including one hit on the rearmost gun turrets of that ship, which set off all the ammunition within these turrets causing a huge fire. However through the valiant efforts of her crew, the fire was extinguished and the terribly damaged *Seydlitz* maintained her speed and position at the head of the German line.

Then it was the turn of the *Lion* to suffer a wounding blow when two shells struck her waterline. Water poured into the engine room, all the electricity failed and the ship had to drop out of the battle line. As Beatty watched his remaining ships steaming past him he sent a somewhat confusing signal '"Attack the rear of the enemy". This was meant to convey the urgency of catching the Germans but was interpreted by Rear Admiral Moore, Beatty's second in command, as an order to concentrated on the unfortunate *Blücher*, now virtually dead in the water far behind the chase. As the British ships turned to finish off the damaged German ship, the rest of Hipper's squadron made their escape. The poor *Blücher* was subjected to a hurricane of fire from the remaining British battlecruisers. She had been hit by at least 70 heavy British shells and 7 torpedoes but she fought to the bitter end, never striking her colours as she slipped beneath the waves at 12. 07pm in the afternoon. The Battle of Dogger Bank was over.

The British public and press hailed Dogger Bank as a great victory but in the Admiralty and amongst senior British admirals, including Beatty himself, the sense of disappointment was palpable, the consensus being that the chance of a great victory had been lost. To some extent Beatty must carry some of the blame and he graciously acknowledged that his signal to engage the enemy rear was open to misinterpretation.

However Beatty's star had never been higher, as Winston Churchill related after the action at Dogger Bank when one of the *Lion*'s officers spoke to him in words of almost religious conviction – "First Sea Lord I have to tell you, Nelson has come again!"

The Battle of Dogger Bank. Bookjacket illustration for *Buller's Dreadnought* by Richard Hough, Little Brown

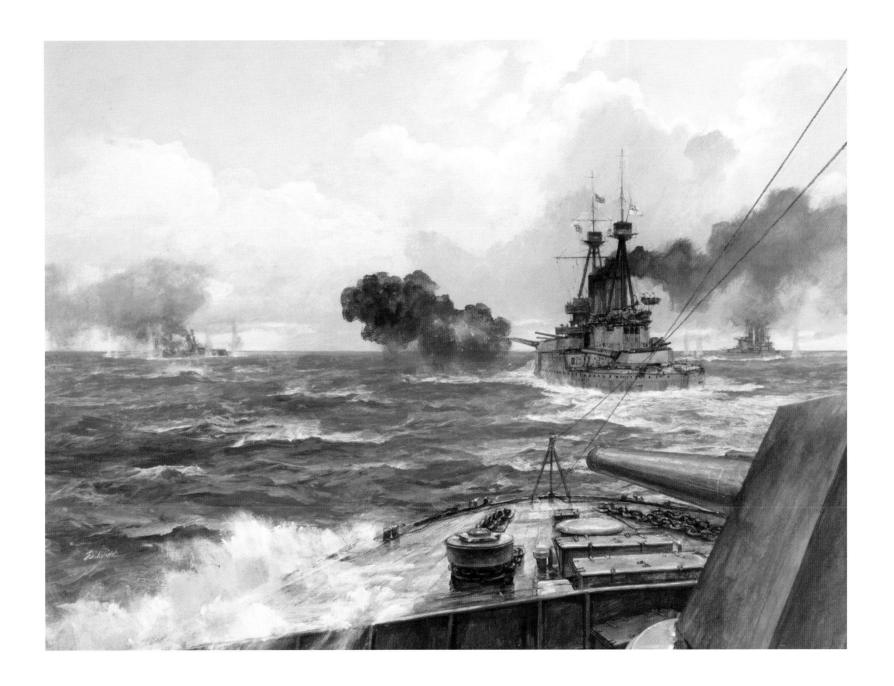

H.M.S. *LION* 1912 British Battlecruiser

Sister ships: *Princess Royal, Queen Mary*

Displacement	26,270 tons
Length	700 ft
Speed	27 knots
Complement	997
Guns	8 - 13.5”, 16 - 4”
Torpedo Tubes	2 - 21”
Armour	9” Hull Belt, 10” Turrets

Following the construction of the battlecruiser *Invincible* and the follow-on New Zealand class, Admiral Fisher was looking for a faster, more powerful successor and in the design of H.M.S. *Lion* he believed he had found it. Mounting heavier guns and more powerful engines producing two extra knots with a greater length and beam H.M.S. *Lion* looked every inch the 'Ocean Greyhound' she was intended to be. Only in her armour was the *Lion* less than a striking improvement on her predecessors.

Such a dashing ship needed an equally dashing commander and in Vice Admiral Sir David Beatty H.M.S. *Lion* had, in the popular imagination, found her 'Nelson', an officer, whose meteoric rise through the ranks of the service had already excited much comment and publicity. With his film-star looks and his prowess in the hunting field and in the highest reaches of society, Beatty was almost typecast in the role of commander of the First Battlecruiser Squadron, the 'eyes' of the fleet.

From his somewhat reckless though successful action against German cruisers in the enemy-controlled Heligoland Bight shortly after the outbreak of the war, Beatty announced his intention to hunt the enemy down wherever he might appear and in whatever strength. So long as the public and some of his officers thought that Beatty was Nelson come again, Beatty was not about to disabuse them.

Beatty and the *Lion*'s next test came at Dogger Bank in early 1915 when in a running fight across the North Sea Beatty sought to destroy Admiral Hipper's battlecruiser squadron. Although inflicting some damage on the enemy, H.M.S. *Lion* was severely damaged herself and had to drop out the line. Owing to confused signals from Beatty the rest of the British line gave up the general chase and turned on the already damaged German cruiser *Blücher* and sank her allowing Hipper to make his escape. A furious Beatty had to be towed back to port.

The really big test was to come at the battle of Jutland where the combined British and German fleets clashed in a monumental gun battle on 31 May, 1916. The action opened appropriately between Beatty's battlecruisers and those of Hipper. Beatty led his 'so called 'Splendid Cats' *Lion*, *Princess Royal*, *Queen Mary*, and *Tiger*, with *New Zealand* and *Indefatigable* bringing up the rear. Very early in the action, H.M.S. *Lion* was hit repeatedly, one shell penetrating the midships turret killing most of its crew and setting it on fire. Lion was in grave danger as the fire raged out of control and but for the heroic action of Major Francis Harvey, Royal Marines, who though mortally wounded ordered the closing of the magazine doors and the flooding of the magazine itself, the ship would have been lost. Major Harvey was posthumously awarded the Victoria Cross.

The furious action continued unabated and soon H.M.S. *Indefatigable* succumbed to devastating gunfire which blew her to pieces killing all but two of her crew. Beatty clung on hitting the German ships again and again but disaster was to repeat itself when H.M.S. *Queen Mary*, the *Lion*'s sister ship became caught in murderous German gunfire and was soon torn apart by three massive explosions. "There seems to be something wrong with our bloody ships today" the laconic Beatty was heard to utter before ordering a closing of the range between the two lines of ships to press the action even harder. Suddenly the whole of the German High Sea's Fleet appeared to the south and Beatty turned north leading the unsuspecting Germans on to the massed guns of Grand Fleet . Beatty, his job done, joined his commander in chief in the pursuit of the fleeing enemy, eventually losing them in the darkness and mists of the oncoming night.

The cost of Jutland was truly terrible, especially to Beatty's battlecruisers whose bravery remains undiminished through the annals of naval warfare.

H.M.S. *Lion* speeds towards battle, oil on canvas, 24 x 36 inches

H.M.S. *Lion* and her dashing commander were instantly compared to H.M.S. *Victory* and Lord Nelson but nothing could disguise the fact that there was something wrong with the British ships that day. They were weaker than their German rivals, their ammunition safety systems were decidedly inferior and as recent dives upon the wrecks have proved, the turrets were literally stuffed with high explosive propellants in order to keep up a continuous discharge of the guns. Such practices may have won the battle of Trafalgar but at Jutland they proved fatal.

Shortly after Jutland, Sir David Beatty became commander of the Grand Fleet, hoisting his flag in H.M.S. *Queen Elizabeth*. H.M.S. *Lion* remained ready to sally forth at the first sight of the enemy but the German fleet never reappeared and by the end of the war the gallant *Lion* was worn out after years of gallant service to her nation. When she was scrapped in 1926, the Nelson spirit of close action with the enemy was no longer an option. Future naval battles would be fought at far greater ranges and a warship's protection and tactics would have to reflect this.

H.M.S. *INVINCIBLE* 2

The complete destruction of Admiral Graf von Spee's armoured cruisers in the south Atlantic by H.M.S. *Invincible* and her sister H.M.S. *Inflexible* proved Admiral Fisher's concept of the battlecruiser as a successful hunter of enemy cruisers and commerce raiders which was the raison d'etre of this novel type of warship. The problem for the battlecruiser was that whilst *Invincible* and her Royal Navy sisters had the oceans to themselves they were unbeatable but when challenged by an enemy possessing ships of a similar speed and power, their supremacy was effectively neutralised, and when in fleet actions against battleships, they were dangerously vulnerable.

By 1914, Germany possessed a fleet of battlecruisers that were to prove superior in almost every respect to their British rivals. With ships of such size and power, the temptation for admirals to involve battlecruisers in fleet actions would prove irresistible.

Battlecruiser commanders such as Beatty, Hood and Hipper were seen as the naval equivalents of dashing cavalry officers, always getting into the thick of the action, drawing the enemy fleets on to the guns of their battleships. In the din of battle, the battlecruiser's original job of hunting down enemy cruisers was easily forgotten; the public looked for the 'Nelson' touch and this meant placing your ships against those of the enemy whatever their strength and power. For the Royal Navy, this misconception of the battlecruiser's role was to lead to terrible tragedy.

The eve of the battle of Jutland, in May 1916, found H.M.S. *Invincible* as the flagship of the 3rd battlecruiser squadron commanded by Admiral Sir Horace Hood attached to the Grand Fleet at Scapa Flow, whilst the 1st Battlecruiser squadron under Admiral Beatty was based further south at Rosyth.

The Battle of Jutland opened with Beatty's battlecruisers hotly engaged with those of Admiral Hipper. Following the loss of two of his ships, Beatty succeeded in bringing the German High Seas Fleet into the arms of the British Grand Fleet. At this point Admiral Hood with *Invincible*, *Inflexible* and *Indomitable* broke station with Admiral Jellicoe's battleships to join Beatty at the head of his depleted squadron. Having severely damaged three German light cruisers, Hood joined battle with the German battlecruisers *Derflinger* and *Lutzow*.

A furious fight developed with *Invincible* firing off volley after volley and scoring numerous hits on the enemy. Then the mists cleared giving the Germans a clear view of Hood's flagship and their gunners quickly found the range. It took one shell to penetrate one of *Invincible*'s midship turrets, touching off the ammunition in the turret which in turn detonated two magazines blowing the proud old ship in two.

When the smoke cleared, H.M.S. *Invincible* was gone, taking all but six of her crew to their deaths including Admiral Hood. The bow and stern stood out from the shallow water marking not only her passing but that of the battlecruiser adventure in the Royal Navy.

H.M.S. *Invincible* leads a heavy cruiser squadron, acrylic on paper, 18.5 x 25 inches

H.M.S. *BARHAM* 1915 British Battleship

Sister ships: *Queen Elizabeth, Warspite, Malaya, Valiant*

Displacement	33,585 tons
Length	646 ft
Speed	25 knots
Guns (1915)	8 - 15", 12 - 6", 2 -3"
Torpedoes	4 - 21" tubes.
Armour	13" belt, 13" Turrets, 3" decks

In 1912 the naval arms race between Britain and Germany was at its height. With an almost endless succession of dreadnought battleships and battlecruisers coming into service in both countries, one large warship begat an even larger one. The largest guns carried on a British capital ship was 13.5" but the Americans and Japanese were commissioning ships with 14" guns and rumours were beginning to circulate that Germany too was planning such ships. The First Lord of the Admiralty, Winston Churchill, decided that the new British battleships of the Queen Elizabeth class should mount even greater guns and after consulting the old naval warlord, Sir John Fisher, they settled on 15", the most powerful ever mounted on a warship.

This decision represented a tremendous leap of faith in British technology and industry as well as an enormous risk. But before any such gun had built and tested, Churchill ordered them into production for the new ships. Another first was to be the use of fuel oil instead of coal. This had many advantages, not least in the ease of refuelling compared with the incredibly messy and time-consuming business of coaling ships.

Another advantage of oil was that it was efficient, enabling a ship to raise steam quickly and to operate at consistently higher speeds than a coal-fired ship. The advocates of coal pointed to the fact that supplies were readily available in the British Isles and its bunkers offered a measure of protection against shell fire. However, as oil is lighter than coal more armour could be built into the ships. Thus it was with H.M.S. *Barham* and her sisters. They were extremely well armoured and because they mounted the heaviest guns they could dispense with one of the turrets, leaving more room for boilers and larger turbines, enabling these large ships to reach 25 knots, easily as fast as a battlecruiser. In the Queen Elizabeth class the Royal Navy at last had ships that did not have to compromise between guns, armour or speed; they had all three in abundance. In May 1916, all of these virtues would be tested to the limit.

Prior to the Battle of Jutland, the commander of the battlecruisers, Admiral Sir David Beatty, requested that the 5th Battle Squadron comprising all the new, fast battleships be placed under his command at Rosyth. The lead ship *Queen Elizabeth* was in dry dock on 31 May when news was received that the German battlecruisers were making their way up to the waters off Jutland on the Danish coast. Beatty immediately set sail, and shortly after Admiral Sir Hugh Evan-Thomas, commanding the 5th Battle Squadron in H.M.S. *Barham,* followed his commander into the North Sea.

When Beatty changed course to shape southwards, a signalling muddle developed and what with the smoke covering the flagship, the signal was not seen on the *Barham* and she and the rest of the 5th Battle Squadron carried on on an easterly course. As a result of this muddle, when Admiral Beatty met the German battlecruisers under the command of Admiral Franz von Hipper, he was denied the vital protection and excellent gunnery afforded by the new battleships. When they finally caught up with Beatty, he was in serious trouble having lost the *Indefatigable* and the *Queen Mary* to the murderous and accurate gun fire of the German ships.

Upon arriving at the running battle southwards, Evan-Thomas' ships immediately made their presence felt, taking Hipper's ships under a deluge of equally accurate and more destructive gunnery and nearly breaking the German line of battle.

At this point, there appeared the whole of the German High Seas Fleet, coming up from the south. Beatty had anticipated this and turned his ships around to lead the Germans north into the arms of the British Grand Fleet bearing down from the north. As before, a signalling muddle developed on Beatty's flagship H.M.S. *Lion* and the messages to Evan-Thomas as to a change of course was confusing and misleading and resulted in the 5th Battle Squadron plunging on southward into a maelstrom of shellfire from all the German ships.

H.M.S. *Barham* being escorted through the Channel, oil on canvas, 30 x 40 inches

As he in turn set a northerly course, Evan-Thomas' flagship, *Barham*, was hit in the forward part of the ship, losing 18 dead and 50 wounded in the process, and serious damage was also done to the *Warspite* and *Malaya*, before they were able to rejoin Beatty.

This battle had amply proved that these new, fast and powerful battleships could not only take punishment but also give it out in large measure. They were in their day, the finest dreadnoughts afloat and were to remain for many years the very best that Britain commissioned into her navy.

THE BIRTH OF THE DESTROYER

The origins of the destroyer, or to give its original name, the 'Torpedo Boat Destroyer' began in the American Civil War where the Confederate semi-submersible boat C.S.S. *Hunley* crashed into the side of a Union warship using a new terrifying device called a spar torpedo. This consisted of a large bomb suspended from a long pole armed with a percussion device. The long pole was supposed to afford the ship some measure of protection from the resulting blast but like the *Hunley*, all to often the attacking ship perished with its target. In spite of the obvious dangers the spar torpedo, and the small relatively fast boats carrying it, found favour in many small navies who saw it as a form of inexpensive (except for the crew) equaliser.

The real revolution came with the Whitehead locomotive torpedo in 1870. Soon torpedo boats carrying this new weapon appeared everywhere, now small navies really did have an equaliser and the newspapers were not slow with lurid depictions of future naval battles where great battleships were humbled by swarms of tiny torpedo boats. In the eyes of the French navy, here was the perfect means to even the score with the all powerful Royal Navy, but the British were not slow to recognise the danger and having commissioned its own torpedo craft, it now searched for an antidote to meet the new menace.

After much trial and not a few errors, they came up with H.M.S. *Havock*. Carrying a 76mm gun, three 47mm guns and three torpedo tubes, *Havock* had genuine attack and defensive capabilities, and at a speed of 26 knots was fast enough to catch any torpedo boat and destroy it.

These early destroyers needed really dedicated and carefully selected crews as the boats were awful to work in, constantly wet, cramped and unventilated, they rattled and bucked in any kind of sea and should they be mishandled in any way, their light construction ensured that they would crumple like paper bags. But these crews developed an *esprit de corps* and a sense of dash and enterprise not allowed their big ship brothers. It is not surprising that many famous admirals sprang from destroyer commands, men like Beatty, Tirpitz, Tovey, Togo and Cunningham.

At 26 knots, the reciprocating engine had reached the limits of its development and at the Jubilee Fleet Review of 1897 this was dramatically demonstrated when the dignified occasion was rudely interrupted by a tiny craft called the *Turbinia*, weaving in and out of the lines of battleships at great speed. It was a demonstration by Sir Charles Parsons of his new steam turbine engine, and whilst the older admirals huffed and puffed at this outrage, the more far-sighted immediately saw the potential in the new means of propulsion, including Sir John Fisher, soon to be First Sea Lord at the Admiralty. He was instrumental in the first use of the steam turbine in the new destroyer H.M.S. *Viper*. When built this ship reached the amazing speed of 36 knots and sustained this over several hours. With H.M.S. *Viper* the pattern of all future destroyers was cast. These hard-hitting small ships were powerful, fast and cheap, and with the rapid advances in technology, they took on more duties including submarine chasing, battlefleet escort, scouting, and latterly, anti-aircraft screening, shore bombardment, radar picket and missile carrier. From a tiny 380-ton ship to the modern 7,000 tonners, the destroyer has come a long way and has undergone a quantum leap in technology and cost. But those early boats set the bar for the daring and courage that has always been the hallmark of the men who have served in destroyers and helped make them the most charismatic of all warships.

H.M.S. *Kempenfelt* in the North Sea, used as the bookjacket: *Look to the Wolves* by Alexander Fullerton (Warner Books), acrylic on board, 15.5 x 23 inches

THE FIRST U-BOAT CAMPAIGN 1914–18

Submarines in 1914 were the most modern and as yet untried weapons of naval warfare. They were small, barely habitable and of very short endurance and their dedicated crews had to develop entirely new tactics to get the best from their novel craft. Opinions varied as to their value and practicality, Admiral Sir John Fisher, that most modern of naval modernisers, was quick to realise the submarine's potential as a silent and invisible ship killer, whilst his arch enemy, the aristocratic Admiral Lord Charles Beresford, probably the most conceited and arrogant officer the Royal Navy ever produced, dismissed the submarine as a "useless plaything" and "Fisher's toys". Others taking the submarine more seriously claimed that these craft were "unfair and damned un-English". The same sort of arguments raged in German naval circles but being all too aware that the German navy could never compete with the Royal Navy in surface warships, the German high command began to see the submarine as a means of redressing the balance between the two rivals without incurring colossal expenditure.

All these arguments were finally put to rest on the morning of 22 September 1914 when three elderly armoured cruisers, H.M.S. *Aboukir*, *Cressy* and *Hogue* arrived at their patrol station off the coast of Holland. The day was brilliantly clear as the cruisers began their patrol in peacetime formation as if they had the sea to themselves. But on that day they did not, for lurking beneath them was the small German coastal submarine U.9 captained by Lt. Otto Weddigan and crewed by 4 officers and 24 men. Weddigan lined up the *Aboukir* and put a torpedo into her causing her to sink almost immediately as her two Sister Ships: raced to her aid. At this moment Weddigan sent two torpedoes crashing into H.M.S. *Hogue* and finally two more into the *Cressy* sinking both within 15 minutes. In little over an hour a tiny submarine had sent three major warships and 1,459 men to their doom. The submarine had come of age.

In both navies the submarine had been seen initially as a fleet support vessel, attacking warships prior to the main surface engagements. However, the effective blockade of Germany by the Royal Navy led the Germans to employ their growing submarine fleet as commerce raiders. This took the form of 'restricted' warfare where an enemy ship was stopped, inspected and its crew allowed to cast-off in lifeboats before their merchant ship was sunk by gunfire.

All this took time and exposed the U-boat to the danger of discovery whilst on the surface, and added to this neutral ships were not to be touched.

Such gentlemanly conduct was ultimately not very effective and robbed the submarine of its greatest assets, invisibility and surprise. Off the south coast of Ireland on the afternoon of 7 May 1915 all this was to change when Captain Walther Schweiger in U.20 sighted the giant ocean liner *Lusitania* making her way to Liverpool with 1,265 passengers and a secret cargo of ammunition and high explosives crammed into her hold for the British war effort. The Germans suspected this and issued warnings in New York that such a liner would be attacked, if found in the war zone around the coasts of Britain, as a legitimate target of war. The warnings were ignored and the ship sailed. As she neared the Irish Sea, Captain Schweiger put one torpedo into the fore part of the liner touching off the ammunition and all but blowing the bows off. R.M.S. *Lusitania* sank within five minutes, taking 1,200 men, women and children to their deaths.

The world-wide outcry nearly bought America into the war at that moment, as many of her citizens perished on the *Lusitania*. This fact, and the negative propaganda the sinking induced, forced Germany to suspend unrestricted submarine warfare for the present, but by 1917 the effects of the British blockade threatened real starvation in Germany and the public clamour to hit back irrespective of American public opinion became irresistible. Unrestricted submarine warfare was resumed in February 1917 and the effects in the first three months was spectacular; 944,000 tons of vital shipping for Britain was sunk and by the end of the year 4 million tons had been sent to the bottom. These losses were so great that a real sense of panic swept through the British Isles. Government estimates considered that if the U-boat went unchecked the Allies would lose the war by November 1917. Somewhat belatedly a convoy system was introduced and, with the newly perfected weapon of depth charging, the German U-boat campaign was eventually defeated but it was a close run thing, too close for all those involved, including a young U-boat captain, Karl Doenitz, who learned the lessons and 24 years later was to launch the next U-boat campaign in the North Atlantic.

U-boat in the North Atlantic, acrylic on board, 21.5 x 14.5 inches

K CLASS STEAM SUBMARINE 1917 British Submarine

Displacement	1,883 Tons
Length	338 ft
Speed	25 knots
Complement	60
Guns	2 - 4" 1 - 3"
Torpedoes	8 - 18"

This is the story of two bad ideas. The first bad idea was the concept of the 'Fleet Submarine', where large submarines formed an integral part of the battlefleet, working in concert with battleships, cruisers and destroyers. The plan was for the submarine to travel on the surface with the fleet until battle was about to be joined. Then they would submerge and attack the enemy with salvoes of torpedoes whilst the battle raged above them. In practice all fleet submarines managed to do was to get in the way of their own ships if they managed to keep up with them at all. The other fleet concept was to entice the enemy out of his bases across a line of waiting submarines who would then fire shoals of torpedoes into them. The usual result of this was lines of submarines waiting in the wrong place, running out of fuel and becoming dangerously exposed to enemy minefields.

The problem with the fleet submarine tactics was that they required perfect co-ordination with the main fleet and the Admiralty and this was never forthcoming. The other problem was that the early submarines were never powerful enough to work with the fleets they were meant to serve. In reality though, the idea of the fleet submarine failed because the submarine was not a battlefleet weapon at all but a perfect commerce raider. The Germans were the first to appreciate this and once they had perfected the ocean-going submarine, they used it with ruthless efficiency, nearly bringing Britain to her knees in the process in 1917. The American navy clung on to the fleet submarine idea until the Pacific war when in imitation of the German 'Wolf Pack' strategy they all but destroyed the Japanese merchant marine. The Japanese never learned the lesson at all and wasted their large submarine fleet in pursuit of useless and complex fleet actions.

As for the British, they had to learn the hard way. Loathed to give up on the fleet submarine they decided to compound a bad idea with an even worse one, the steam submarine. Even Admiral Fisher, that man of novel and sometimes implausible ideas, saw the implausibility of a submarine powered by steam, but his scepticism was swept aside in the fever generated in Whitehall to make the fleet submarine concept work.

The K class submarines were enormous, the size of a light cruiser, weighing in at 1,833 tons apiece and powered on the surface by a pair of oil-fired boilers, giving them a surface speed of 25 knots. Four electric motors were used when submerged and a back-up diesel engine was employed whilst waiting for the boiler pressure to build up.

In order to dive, the fires had to be drawn, the smoke cleared, the ventilators closed and the funnels collapsed into the hull before no less than eleven watertight hatches were closed. All this took a minimum of four minutes to achieve whereas a conventional submarine crashed dived in 30 seconds. As one K Boat officer put it "They simply had too many holes". They were also too big to handle effectively, being described as having a turning circle of a battlecruiser. The were also in the habit of diving spontaneously; on one of these dives the boat plunged to the bottom, digging into the shallow water and taking with her the future King George VI . Having been rescued, the future monarch took up flying instead. After all the mishaps during their trials, the real 'dark night of the soul' for the K Boats came on the night of 1 February 1918 when 9 of these craft were involved in the so called 'Battle of May Island'. A badly-planned nighttime exercise involving 9 K Boats got underway off the north coast of Scotland, with submarines keeping station in the midst of units of the Grand Fleet, all of them going at full speed. Unfortunately some minesweepers swept across in front of the formation of K Boats forcing them to take violent evasive action. The chaos that ensued has gone down in history as the worst debacle involving submarines ever recorded. In their haste to avoid colliding with the minesweepers the unwieldy K Boats collided with each other and other vessels coming up from behind. The carnage was indescribable, submarines were cut in half, two of them sank and all were damaged, and 103 brave men lost their lives uselessly.

But in spite of this, the British were still reluctant to let the idea of the fleet submarine go and converted two K Boats into 'Battleship Submarines', mounting one 12" gun which could fire above and below the surface. One of these was lost in collision with a merchant ship in the English Channel whilst another K Boat was converted to carry an aeroplane. This was also lost when the crew failed to close the hanger door when diving. After this, the British quietly bought the curtain down on their story of the fleet submarine.

In all, 322 men were lost on the K Boats, none of them to enemy action.

K15 at Sea - an illustration from calendar: 'Strange and Innovative Ships', B.P. Marine

H.M.S. *HOOD* 1920-1941 British Battleship/Battlecruiser

Displacement	45,314 tons (full load)
Length	860 ft
Speed	32 knots
Complement	1,500
Guns	8 - 15". 12 - 5.5". 4 - 4"
Torpedoes	6 - 21"
Armour	12" Hull belt 12" Turrets

In the long history of warships there have been vessels whose exploits have earned them an enduring affection and admiration throughout the world. H.M.S. *Victory*, U.S.S. *Constitution*, I.J.N. *Mikasa*, U.S.S. *Missouri*, all have played their part in their respective nations' glories and all still exist to be admired. Like heroes in an opera, they have played their respective roles and have triumphed, leaving the stage garlanded and applauded down through the ages. But opera also contains the stuff of tragedy, the very symmetry of disaster where the beautiful hero or heroine sings their way gloriously and inevitably to their doom.

In 1915, intelligence reports reaching the British Admiralty told of a new class of German battlecruisers being built which would outclass any existing Royal Navy ships of this type. To counter this, a new 'Admiral' class of four great battlecruisers was designed and laid down. However, following the disastrous performance of this kind of ship in the battle of Jutland in 1916, the Royal Navy instructed the designers of the new ships to recast their plans taking into account the lessons learned in the recent battle. The new design called for fast battleships armoured and gunned to the level of the successful Queen Elizabeth class but with speeds well in excess of the 25 knots these ships were capable of.

In order to achieve the performance required, the new ships would have to be of such a length and displacement as to accommodate the massively increased engine and boiler equipment needed to drive such ships to speeds of a least 30 knots.

Where as the *Queen Elizabeth*'s overall length was 645 ft on a tonnage of 33, 548 tons, the new 'Admirals' would weigh in at 45,314 tons on a length of 860 ft. Such a quantum leap in tonnage and power bought with it new problems, the new ships would have to be very long and the armour would have to be spread across this length upon ships with a relatively shallow draught.

Inevitably sacrifices had to be made and thus the level of deck armour had to be drastically reduced. This was ultimately to prove a fatal flaw in an otherwise brilliant design. Then, further intelligence reached the Admiralty that the Germans had abandoned the building of their new ships in order to concentrate on submarine production. This in turn led the Admiralty to cancel three of their new 'Admirals' but the forth, H.M.S. *Hood*, was too far advanced so she alone was completed and launched by the widow of Admiral Sir Horace Hood who lost his life on the battlecruiser *Invincible* at Jutland.

As completed in 1920, H.M.S. *Hood* completely captured the imagination of the British public and admirers of the Royal Navy throughout the world. In the opinion of many she was and still is the most dramatically beautiful warship ever to sail the seas.

Where as all capital ships manifested a kind of stout and latent power, H.M.S. *Hood* added a unique grace of line and proportion worthy of an ocean liner. Throughout the twenty-odd years of her busy life, she visited every major port in the United Kingdom where the ship was thrown open to the public. Many romances blossomed during the dances and parties held on her decks (including a lady who bought an early painting from the author as a memory of where she had met her future husband). And these parties and entertainments continued around the world which she circumnavigated several times during her various commissions. Slated for a complete modernisation during the 1930s H.M.S. *Hood* was proving too valuable a unit of the fleet, and the amount of goodwill she generated abroad as well as at home continued to put back her modernisation. In 1939, when a final date had been set, the dockyard in her home port of Portsmouth had been made ready when war broke out and she was called to Scapa Flow to join the Home Fleet. The 'Mighty *Hood*' was feted never to be modernised and thus this beautiful and much loved ship never lost her looks, sailing into the Second World war almost unchanged.

H.M.S. *Hood*, oil on board, 24 x 36 inches

U.S.S. *TENNESSEE* 1920 U.S. Battleship

Sister ship: *California*

Displacement	32,300 tons
Dimensions	624 ft
Speed	21 knots
Complement	1,083
Guns	12 - 14", 14 - 5", 4 - 3"
Torpedo Tubes	2 - 21"
Armour	14" belt, 18" turrets.

"A gun crew from every Tennessee town" ran the 1920 recruiting slogan calling for volunteers from all over Tennessee to man the latest U.S. battleship named for the famous southern state.

U.S.S. *Tennessee* and her sister *California* differed from contemporary foreign dreadnought designs in several important respects, the most obvious being the employment of the 'cage' mast, a distinctly American design feature which was strong enough to carry the increasingly heavy and complex fire control platforms yet light enough not to compromise the stability of the ship. The same geodetic structures were used by the English aircraft designer Barnes Wallis in the famous Wellington bomber, and they have been a feature of engineering and architectural design ever since. The next novel feature was to place the battleship's secondary armament above the main deck where at least it would be dry and have some measure of usefulness when bought to battle in the roughest seas. Inside the *Tennessee* the engines were also a design first, being turbo-electric, this meant placing powerful electric motors between the steam turbines and the propellor shafts, thus doing away with heavy reversing turbines and giving the ships a fair amount of manoeuvrability by directly controlling the speed of the electric drive. Finally, U.S.S. *Tennessee* employed a system of armour protection which was copied all over the world. This was the so-called 'all or nothing' principal which involved heavily armouring the vital parts of the ship, the turrets, conning tower, the magazines and the engines and nothing else. Prior to this design feature, armour plating was scattered all over the ships with the inevitable compromises and weaknesses of trying to do too much within a limited tonnage. This meant that *Tennessee* and all her American successors were heavily armoured where it mattered. Finally these ships were the last to mount the highly efficient American 14" gun, after them all U.S. battleships would be armed with 16" guns.

On 7 December 1941 U.S.S. *Tennessee* and her sister *California* were moored with the other American dreadnoughts of the Pacific Fleet at Pearl Harbor when the Japanese carrier planes attacked. Hit by two bombs and severely damaged by debris and fire when U.S.S. *Arizona* blew up directly astern of her, *Tennessee* was spared the torpedo hits suffered by her sister, being inboard of U.S.S. *West Virginia* which sank at her moorings trapping the *Tennessee*. She was only saved from the flames raging all round her by the valiant efforts of her crew before being freed from the inferno.

Following extensive reconstruction on the United States west coast shipyards, U.S.S. *Tennessee* emerged transformed into a new battleship, her appearance completely changed, the only part of the old ship remaining were the guns and her hull which was considerably widened to carry extensive anti-aircraft batteries.

During her war service, U.S.S. *Tennessee* won many citations for her formidable fire support during the island-hopping campaigns carried out by the U.S. Marine Corps right across the Pacific. She bombarded the beachheads of Tarawa, New Ireland, Saipan, Tinian, Guam, Palau, Leyte, Iwo Jima and Okinawa. As well as these epic battles, *Tennessee* took part in the last naval battle between battleships when, with other veterans of the Pearl Harbor attack, she helped sink the Japanese battleships *Fuso* and *Yamashiro* in the Surigao Strait during the battle of Leyte Gulf.

Her last battles were with Kamikaze attackers off Okinawa were she was hit by one of them which caused local but extensive damage, suffering 25 killed and 104 wounded in the ensuing explosion and fire. Fully repaired she proudly took her place at the Japanese surrender before going into retirement. 'Mothballed' for several years the brave old *Tennessee* was finally towed away for scrapping in 1959.

U.S.S. Tennessee, acrylic on paper, 18 x 25 inches

H.M.S. *RODNEY* 1927 British Battleship

Sister ship: *Nelson*

Displacement	(full load) 38,000 tons.
Length	710 ft (216 m)
Beam	106 ft (32m)
Speed	23 knots
Complement	1640
Guns	9 - 16", 12 - 6", 6 - 4.7", 8 - 4" AA, 48 pom pom AA.
Torpedo	Tubes 2 - 24.5"
Armour	Hull Belt 14", Decks 6.25", Turrets 16"

H.M.S. *Rodney* and her sister ship H.M.S. *Nelson* were the first 'Washington Treaty' battleships to be built following the famous treaty signed between the major maritime nations in 1922. This bought to an end a potentially dangerous and ruinously expensive arms race between Britain, the U.S.A. and Japan. Huge battleships and battlecruisers were already on the stocks and some nearing completion when the U.S. government proposed an arms limitation treaty (the first of its kind) which resulted in a 'Battleship Holiday'. This meant that no new battleships could be added to the major powers' fleets for 10 years, and many older existing ships were to be scrapped. However America and Japan had already commissioned 16"-gunned battleships and much of the Royal Navy's ships had been worn out by continuous war service, so the British were allowed to build two ships up to the treaty limits of 35,000 tons (unladen).

Any warship is a balance of firepower, armour and speed, and the British designers realised that to mount the heaviest guns and the thickest armour required a reduction of speed in order to remain within the treaty limits. Thus the *Rodney* and *Nelson* with a maximum speed of 23 knots were amongst the slowest modern capital ships built. In order to shorten the amount of heavy armour employed to protect the guns, magazines and engines, the nine 16" guns in their three turrets were grouped together forward of the streamlined bridge giving the ships an unusual and somewhat ugly appearance. In fact it can be said that the designer, Sir Eustace Tennyson D'eyncourt had created the first 'modernist' battleship. With its angularity and uncompromising appearance *Rodney* seemed to belong to the world of modern art and 'brutalist' architecture. The irony is that the same designer helped create H.M.S. *Hood* whose grace and beauty certainly proved that D'eyncourt was, as a naval architect, certainly also an artist. But with his next designs, *Rodney* and *Nelson*, he was an artist prepared to throw away his own rule book.

Such a radical design bought about several problems, not least the blast pressure damage to the bridge when the main armament was fired. As well as this, with all of the weight of the turrets grouped together, the ship was difficult to handle. The joke that went around the fleet concerning the *Rodney* and *Nelson*, 'My end's turning to starboard, what's your end doing?', had a measure of truth about it, but such big ships were not destroyers so a more stately if somewhat erratic progress was acceptable. Most battleships carried their main armament divided fore and aft to discourage a potentially chasing enemy. However this was not seen as a problem for these two ships which, with their slow speed, could never outrun an enemy, and with their massive guns and armour they were designed to 'slug it out' with any potential opponent. And in 1941, H.M.S. *Rodney*'s opponent was no less than the *Bismarck*, seen at the time as the greatest battleship afloat. *Rodney*'s shooting was remarkably accurate from the outset and by the end of the duel she had advanced to within 4000 yards of the *Bismarck*, firing broadsides at point blank range and reducing the German ship to a shambles. The only damage to the *Rodney* was from the blast of her own guns. Further war service included Malta and Russian convoys and fire support for the Sicily and especially Normandy landings. Off the Normandy coast *Rodney* became feared by the German defenders; her deadly fire was so accurate that whole German tank battalions and troops massing to attack the allies were destroyed. The captured Germans admitted that *Rodney*'s guns had done more to break their morale then any amount of fighting.

By 1945 the proud old ship was completely worn out, so she was placed in reserve before joining her sister in the breaker's yard in 1948.

H.M.S. *Rodney* was an odd looking ship but a stout one and a worthy opponent to the best that any country could throw at her, and many both on land and sea were glad and grateful for her service.

H.M.S. *Rodney*, acrylic on paper, 15 x 20 inches

I.J.N. *ASHIGARA* 1929 Japanese Heavy Cruiser

Sister ships: *Myoko, Nachi, Haguro*

Displacement	15,993 tons
Dimensions	668 ft
Speed	33 knots
Complement	970
Guns	10 - 8", 8 - 5", 8+ - 1" AA
Torpedo tubes	16 - 24 Long Lance + 8 reloads
Armour	4" belt, 1.4" decks
Aircraft	3

The story of Japanese warship and especially cruiser design of the interwar period is very much the story of two brilliant men, Yuzuro Hiraga, the chief of naval construction, and his assistant Kikuo Fujimoto. It would not be putting it too highly to say that these two, especially Hiraga were the greatest warship designers of their day. The fact was that all warship designers throughout the twenties and thirties closely studied what was being produced in Japan, revising their plans to accommodate the lessons of that country's latest thinking.

The first product of this partnership was the experimental light cruiser I.J.N. *Yubari* which became the progenitor of all subsequent Japanese cruisers. Up until *Yubari* the standard cruiser design was a compromise between offence and defence, guns and torpedoes versus armour and speed. Bigger guns and more armour meant a slower ship, unless larger engines were used which meant increasing the size of the ship. This in turn meant an increased tonnage resulting in a slower speed again. In designing the *Yubari* Hiraga and Fujimoto decided to square this particular circle. The method they chose was to keep the weight down without sacrificing the armour protection. They achieved this by making the armour part of the ship's structure instead of the usual practice of hanging armour on to the structure of the hull. The result of this revolutionary idea was to reduce the tonnage drastically whilst greatly strengthening the overall construction. The benefits of this were increased speed and armament on a reduced tonnage and, along with a completely new hull design, *Yubari* was a fantastically efficient warship. And then there was the added dimension of the Washington Naval Disarmament conference which set a limit on the tonnage of a heavy cruiser to 10,000 tons.

Hiraga and Fujimoto designed two more classes of medium cruisers before embarking on their first 10,000 ton 'Washington' cruiser the *Ashigara*. This ship and her three sisters was as revolutionary as the earlier *Yubari* had been.

Heavily armed with ten 8' guns, aircraft and heavy AA artillery, they were better armoured than their American counterparts, and faster. Added to this these new cruisers were equipped with a new and deadly weapon, the 'Long Lance' 24" oxygen-fuelled torpedo. Whilst other navies had tried to harness the obvious potential of oxygen as a propellant for their torpedoes, the Japanese had secretly perfected the weapon. The advantages were greater speed and destructive power, the huge 'Long Lance' could disable a battleship with one hit and blow a cruiser in half . This was proved in the early battles of the Pacific war when many allied ships were lost to this sinister weapon. However, such an advantage as the Japanese navy enjoyed with this new, powerful tool came at a price. To maximise its battle potential meant that Japanese cruisers were crammed full of torpedoes. *Ashigara* carried twenty-four and some cruisers even more. The potential for disaster was obvious, one unlucky bomb hit in the torpedo room with torpedoes filled with volatile fuel and high explosive could shatter and sink a cruiser, and during the war the Japanese navy lost ten heavy cruisers to this cause.

In 1937 *Ashigara* represented her country at the Coronation Fleet Review of King George VI and created much comment and interest , with her sleek lines and heavy armament the Japanese cruiser seemed to be the very epitome of grace and power.

However one Royal Navy officer loudly offered his opinion on the visitor from the Far East. "Very pretty but not a proper warship"! Time would tell.

During the war in the Pacific, *Ashigara* participated in the conquest of the Philippines, and she helped sink the Cruiser H.M.S. *Exeter*, and the destroyers H.M.S. *Encounter* and U.S.S. *Pillbury* in the battle of the Java Sea. And it was in these waters that *Ashigara* spent most of her war protecting the Japanese conquest of the Dutch East Indies. However, she also participated in the

I.J.N. *Ashigara*, acrylic on paper, 15 x 22 inches

disastrous Battle of Surigao Strait where the two battleships she was escorting, *Fuso* and *Yamashiro* were sunk, along with her sister cruiser *Nachi*.

Ashigara returned to her old patrolling grounds off Sumatra in June 1945 when she was hit by no less than five torpedoes from the British submarine H.M.S. *Trenchant* and rapidly sank. *Exeter* and *Encounter* had been avenged in the same waters where they had been lost four years before.

I.J.N. *TAKAO* 1932 Japanese Heavy Cruiser

Sister ships: *Chokai, Atago, Maya*

Displacement	15,875 tons
Dimensions	668 ft
Speed	34 knots.
Complement	970
Armament	10 - 8", 8 - 5", 24 - 1"
Torpedo tubes	16 - 24" + 8 reloads
Aircraft	2 - 3
Armour	5" belt, 1.4" deck

These successors to the *Ashigara* class was designed by Kikuo Fujimoto in the absence of his superior Juzura Hiraga who was studying shipbuilding trends in England. When he returned to Japan Hiraga approved the designs but warned against the trend of the naval staff demanding more and more guns and torpedo equipment and their ancillary range finders from ships of a limited displacement thus causing stability problems. Within a short time he was proved correct when Fujimoto-designed ships began either capsizing or, in the case of the *Takao*'s successor cruisers, literally coming apart at the (welded) seams. These problems well illustrated the differences between these two revolutionary naval architects; Hiraga, the 'master' would brook no opposition to his design concepts from whatever quarter, whereas Fujimoto was far more susceptible to pressure from the naval staffs whose unrealistic demands overstepped what was technically possible. The result of these failings was that the gifted but pliable Fujimoto was dismissed from his post, whilst the 'master', Hiraga went on to design his magnum opus, the giant battleship *Yamato*.

Although *Takao* embodied most of the Hiraga design principals, her most distinctive feature was the huge armoured 'pagoda' style bridge containing all the complex range finding and other equipment suited to role of the fleet flagships, which they were designed to be.

The resulting stability problems arising from this meant that the ships had to be extensively modified with reduced bridge structures and large torpedo bulges to make them more stable. As a result of these modifications, *Takao* and two of her sisters (*Chokai* was never modified) became extremely efficient and fast heavy cruisers and easily a match for any foreign rivals.

All these vessels had very busy war services, but *Takao*'s moment of glory came on the night of 15 November 1942 when, in concert with her sister *Atago*

and the battleship *Kirishima*, along with several light cruisers and destroyers, she travelled down the 'slot' which separated Guadalcanal from the other Solomon Islands. That night the American battleships *South Dakota* and *Washington,* with attendant destroyers, were sailing towards them, although neither side had spotted the other until they met almost head on. The Americans had the advantage of radar, but the Japanese had developed their night fighting tactics to a very high level and both sides spotted each other almost simultaneously.

The Japanese struck first sinking two U.S. destroyers, then the *South Dakota* shattered a Japanese destroyer and in doing so exposed herself to the Japanese heavy forces creeping up on her. At this vital juncture her radar failed and the battleship was virtually blind when she was illuminated by searchlights from the *Kirishima, Takao* and *Atago*. All three Japanese ships opened a withering fire on the *South Dakota* hitting her with 27 large calibre shells, wrecking the bridge and disabling one of her main turrets. Fires were burning out of control when she staggered out of line thus in turn exposing the Japanese ships to the unseen *Washington* following her. This time it was the Japanese who were to suffer when the *Kirishima* was reduced to a blazing wreck by a rain of 16" shells. *Takao* and *Atago* vainly tried to defend the *Kirishima* but in the end she had to be abandoned to her fate as the Japanese withdrew.

Takao continued operations around the Solomon Islands before being struck by a 500lb bomb requiring repairs in Japan. More escort patrols followed until by October 1944 the war had so markedly turned against the Japanese, and the Philippines had become so threatened that the High Command decided on a massive operation involving almost the entire navy in

I.J.N. *Takao*, acrylic on paper, 17 x 25 inches

an effort to prevent the landings taking place in the Gulf of Leyte. *Takao* was in the main body of the fleet when she was struck by two torpedoes and severely damaged. The stricken cruiser barely made it back to her base and following repairs was eventually sent to Singapore to act as an anti-aircraft guardship. And it was in this capacity on the 31 July 1945 that British X Craft midget

submarines found and attacked her, effectively disabling the ship and putting her out of commission permanently. For this courageous exploit the commander of the X Craft Lt. I.E. Fraser was awarded the Victoria Cross.

One year later *Takao*, the last of the famous Japanese heavy cruisers was towed out to sea by the British and scuttled off Singapore Island.

K.M. *ADMIRAL GRAF SPEE* 1933 German Armoured Cruiser

Sister ships: *Admiral Sheer, Deutschland (Lutzow)*

Displacement	15,900 tons full load
Length	610 ft
Speed	26 knots
Complement	950
Armament	6 - 11", 8 - 5.9", 6 - 8.8cm
Torpedoes	8 - 21" tubes
Aircraft	2
Armour	2.36" - 3" belt, 1.6"decks, 5.5" turrets

The Treaty of Versailles of 1919, banned Germany from operating an ocean going navy. Any capital ships were not to exceed 10,000 tons and were only to provide replacements for the ancient pre-dreadnought battleships she had been allowed to retain from her once mighty navy. This provided a real challenge to the planners of the new German navy, the first old ship was due to be replaced at the end of the 1920s yet to keep within the treaty limits, the new designs would have to be dramatically innovative.

Many designs were drawn up which tried to square the circle relating to the competing claims of endurance, speed, gun power and armour on a limited displacement.   The design that finally emerged was ingenious and owed more than a little to Admiral Sir John Fisher's dictum which he applied to his brainchild, the battlecruiser, "Faster than the most powerful battleship, more powerful than the fastest cruiser". The German designers gave their new creations six 11" guns fore and aft and eight 5.5" cannons ranged along her armoured sides, whilst a powerful suite of eight torpedo tubes were mounted on her stern.

All of this was achieved on the nominal displacement of 10,000 tons, although all three vessels were well overweight when completed. Still the maritime world was surprised and intrigued when the statistics of these ships were revealed. The British press immediately christened them 'Pocket Battleships' although the Germans never acknowledged this title, to them, *Admiral Graf Spee* and her sisters were 'Panzerschiffes' or armoured cruisers.

In order to save weight, the extensive use of electric welding, a new technology in shipbuilding in the 1930s, replaced rivets. Mounting the main armament in two triple turrets also bought the tonnage down, but the most revolutionary aspects of these ships was their powerful MAN diesel engines, the biggest ever mounted in a ship up to that time.

These engines had many advantages over the more conventional steam turbines not least in their range of 9,000 miles before refuelling, nearly twice that of turbine-powered ships. Another advantage was the ability to accelerate remarkably quickly, thus being able to outrun most opponents.

There were also some disadvantages to this novel form of propulsion; they were noisy, they were heavy and took up too much space, and they were prone to vibrations, often upsetting the delicate fire control systems. Engines could not be replaced very easily on account of their size. It was of little surprise that no other navy followed the German lead in putting diesels into their largest warships and in the German shipyards themselves, this experiment was not to be repeated except in submarines.

These armoured cruisers were never meant to be 'ships of the line' but the German navy found that with their great range, they would be ideally suited to the role of commerce raiders, hiding in the vast oceans near the shipping lanes and falling upon enemy merchant ships using the elements of surprise and disguise before disappearing again like ghosts from the sea. Just prior to the outbreak of war, the head of the Reich's navy Admiral Erich Reader dispatched his commerce raiders in the north and south Atlantic along with a well organised supply chain of tankers and merchant ships to await the call to arms. When this came in September 1939, *Graf Spee* and the other 'pocket battleships' were ready.

K.M. *Admiral Graf Spee*, used as the bookjacket: *The Battle of the River Plate*, Michael Powell, New English Library, watercolour-tempera, 17.5 x 23 inches

K.M. *SCHARNHORST* 1936 German Battleship

Sister ship: *Gneisenau*

Displacement	34,840 tons
Length	753 ft
Speed	31 knots
Complement	1968
Guns	9 - 11, 12 - 5.9", 14 - 4.1
Torpedo Tubes	6 - 21"
Aircraft	4
Armour	13.8" Belt. 14" Turrets

Named after the two famous, gallant armoured cruisers in the First World War, the fast battleships *Scharnhorst* and *Gneisenau* were launched in the presence of Adolf Hitler in 1936, two months after he had renounced the Treaty of Versailles and marched into the Rhineland. As powerful statements of Germany's emerging power and technical advancement, the building of these two warships was designed to be a showcase to the rest of the world of the new Germany, and also a warning.

More specifically the new German ships were designed as a counter to the modern French battlecruisers *Dunkerque* and *Strasbourg* which in their turn were built to counter the so called 'pocket battleships' of the German navy. Given their announced 26,000 ton displacement and their 11" main armament, the *Scharnhorst* and *Gneisenau* were considered by the rest of the world to be battlecruisers, but as the real displacement was much higher these well-armoured ships were to all intents and purposes fast battleships.

During their design much debate centred around the size of their guns. Hitler wanted his new ships to mount six 15" guns but as these weapons were in the development stage the German navy persuaded him that in order to get the ships quickly into commission nine of the tried and tested 11" would be a suitable alternative, with the proviso that the mountings would be built to adapt to 15" guns when they came on stream.

As built the ships were found to be very 'wet' in any kind of sea, so they were soon back in the shipyards where they were given new 'Atlantic' bows and funnel caps. These changes endowed *Scharnhorst* and *Gneisenau* with a graceful beauty unmatched by any other German ship, although these changes failed to solve the problem of sea spray, and the ships remained extremely 'wet' throughout their service.

The *Scharnhorst* and *Gneisenau* were designed as commerce raiders and as such, the two ships operated together for most of their careers, in fact they seemed so inseparable that the Royal Navy christened them 'Salmon and Gluckstein' after the founders of a famous department store. And together *Scharnhorst* and *Gneisenau* enjoyed considerable success, sinking 22 merchant ships, the aircraft carrier *Glorious* and the destroyers *Ardent* and *Acasta* during the Norwegian campaign. Following these successes, both ships were sent to Brest for refit and repair and it was there that they received almost constant attention from the R.A.F. during which *Scharnhorst* was damaged by bombs. With their new base becoming increasingly like a prison, Hitler took the bold decision to bring the ships back to Germany through the most hazardous route - the English Channel. In making his decision Hitler gambled on the fact that the British would not be expecting such a bold move right under their noses and would not be prepared to counter it. In this he was proved correct; the ships carried out their voyage through mainly daylight hours yet they were not spotted until they had nearly reached the Straits of Dover, by then it was too late to effect serious co-ordinated counter measures. Despite the extraordinary gallantly shown by the Swordfish and Beaufort torpedo planes sent out to stop the ships, the aircraft were shot out of the sky almost to a man. The torpedo boats fared little better whilst high level bombers missed their targets completely. In short, the British reaction to 'Operation Thunderbolt' was botched from start to finish, the *Scharnhorst* and *Gneisenau* reaching their German ports by nightfall. The only damage was to *Scharnhorst* which hit a couple of mines, and these had probably been laid by the Germans themselves.

From this point, the sisters parted company. Two weeks later the R.A.F. attacked *Gneisenau* in her port of Kiel and damaged her so badly that she took

K.M. Scharnhorst, oil on canvas, 24 x 36 inches

no more part in the war. *Scharnhorst* was moved to northern Norway to join the battleship *Tirpitz* and various cruisers to form a 'fleet in being' to threaten the Russian convoys and to tie down the heavy units of the Home Fleet. Apart from an ineffective raid on the deserted island of Spitsbergen, the 'fleet in being' led a fairly quiet life until late December 1943 when *Scharnhorst* emerged to attack convoy JW 55B on its way to Murmansk. Due to bad weather and faulty intelligence the Germans were unaware that ahead of the convoy steamed a Royal Navy battle group which included the battleship *Duke of York*, the cruisers *Belfast, Sheffield, Jamaica* and *Norfolk*, with four destroyers, the fleet being commanded by Admiral Sir Hugh Fraser. Tracking the *Scharnhorst* by radar, the cruisers suddenly illuminated the German ship and subjected her to a hail of 8" gunfire, disabling her radar and communications systems. Then the *Duke of York* moved in for the kill with devastating radar-directed gunfire which stopped the *Scharnhorst* in her tracks. Finally the cruisers and destroyers fired at least 13 torpedoes into the stately battleship before she blew up and sank, taking with her all but 36 of her crew. In the spirit of her proud namesake, the *Scharnhorst* did not strike her colours but in those terrible icy seas, fought to the very end.

H.M.S. *BELFAST* 1938 British Cruiser

Sister ship: *Edinburgh*

Displacement	10,000 tons
Length	613 ft
Speed	32 knots
Complement	850
Guns	12 - 6", 12 - 4", 16 - 6 pdr AA, 8 - 0.5" AA
Armour	4" belt, 2" deck, 2" turrets
torpedoes	6 - 21" tubes.
Aircraft	3

The genesis of the British Town class cruisers began far away in Japan, where their inventive naval designers unveiled the Mogami class 'light' cruisers. The word 'light' was something of a misnomer when applied to these ships as they were exceptionally heavily armed with 15 - 6" guns on a nominal displacement of 850 tons. Even if this tonnage was correct (which it wasn't), the facts and figures of these new ships startled navies all over the world. What the world did not know was that on their sea trials the Japanese discovered that their designers had overreached themselves, the ships being massively top heavy and the welding of large portions of the ship's structure began to fail drastically. The ships had to be returned to dock and virtually rebuilt.

Be that as it may, the American and British naval architects and planners soon came up with their replies to the Japanese threat, the American Brooklyn class and the British Towns. In the British ships, their designers realised that the Japanese figures didn't add up and their new ships would have to be at least 10,000 tons each and to carry any sort of protection at all, would have to sacrifice one turret. As built the Towns were strong and well-balanced cruisers especially the *Belfast* and *Edinburgh* which were built to a somewhat different design to the others, having their internal machinery and magazine spaces rearranged giving the two ships a slightly awkward profile compared to their more pleasing sisters.

With their comprehensive protection and heavy armament, H.M.S. *Belfast* and *Edinburgh* were among the best of their type anywhere, in a world steadily marching to war. Very soon these very qualities of strength would be tested when on 21 November, *Belfast* struck a magnetic mine in the Firth of Forth causing immense damage to the ship and breaking her back. She spent the next two years virtually being rebuilt with even more strength being added to her hull. By the time *Belfast* re-entered service, her sister had already been lost

carrying Russian gold repayments back to Britain when she was torpedoed. H.M.S. *Belfast*, carried on her sister's convoy protection duties to Russia and back and it was on one of these runs in December 1943 that *Belfast* played a leading role in the Battle of the North Cape. Signals had been received that the German battlecruiser *Scharnhorst* was closing on an east-bound convoy to Murmansk. *Belfast* and the heavy cruiser *Norfolk* moved to intercept and picked up the German ship on *Belfast*'s radar. Action was soon joined and telling hits were made on the *Scharnhorst* which once again vanished into the darkness. *Belfast* and *Norfolk* closed on the convoy again in anticipation that *Scharnhorst* would make another try and sure enough *Belfast* picked her up again on her radar. This time the convoy had the support of the Battleship *Duke of York* and *Belfast* directed her to the German raider. To the burst of star shells, a terrific battle ensued between all the ships before the blazing *Scharnhorst* was blown up with the loss of almost all her crew. Thus ended the last ship-to-ship action in the European war.

The Battle of the North Cape was not the last action that *Belfast* would see as she was called upon to shell the German positions on the Normandy beachhead during D Day in June 1944. When the war ended in 1945, *Belfast* had five years of peace before she was in action again off the Korean coast, shelling enemy divisions in support of the allied landings there.

H.M.S. *Belfast* finally ended her long active duty in 1963 when she was paid off into the reserve fleet. Finally as the scrapyard beckoned, a committee was formed in order to save her as a museum ship and memorial to the modern navy. Happily, after a lot of hard work from many dedicated individuals, H.M.S. *Belfast* was saved for the nation and is now part of the Imperial War Museum, berthed at Tower Bridge and visited by thousands each year, a proud old ship and the last of her kind of cruiser anywhere in the world.

H.M.S. *Belfast*, acrylic on paper, 15 x 22 inches

K.M. *BISMARCK* 1940 German battleship

Sister ship: *Tirpitz.*

Displacement	50,153 tons. (full load)
Length	823 ft
Speed	30 knots
Complement	2,098
Guns	8 - 15", 18 - 5.9", 16 - 4.1" AA
Armour	12.6" belt , 14" turrets
Aircraft	6

To those who are specifically interested in naval affairs, certain ships stand out for their epoch-making technology, or the part they played in history. Ships such as *Victory, Monitor, Dreadnought, Invincible, Missouri* are writ large across the pages of naval developments. However to the general public the word 'battleship' means only one thing - *Bismarck*. This iconic warship has come to represent massive strength, terrifying power and near invincibility. Many people who have little idea who Chancellor Otto von Bismarck was will certainly know of the battleship that bore his name. With the weight of mythology that surrounds this ship it is perhaps useful to bring some perspective to her design, her intended function and her very short life.

The battleship *Bismarck* was one of the first of the 'super' dreadnoughts which included the Japanese *Yamato*, the U.S. *Missouri* and the Italian *Vittorio Venito* which all came into service at more or less the same time. Whilst all these latter ships enjoyed the fruits of ongoing naval developments and technology, the German designers were denied direct access to these improvements as a result of the Versailles Treaty. Thus the Germans had to fall back on the basic design philosophies of First World War ships, most specifically their largest battleship *Baden*, built in 1915. The hull design of this ship was enlarged and streamlined but her armoured deck was positioned lower in the ship than those of her contemporaries thus exposing her communication spaces and range-finding computers to possible battle damage. As with the older design her steering gear and rudders did not enjoy enough protection and unlike those modern ships in foreign navies her secondary armament did not have anti-aircraft capability, separate AA turrets and guns being fitted and adding to the overall weight of the ship.

On the plus side, whilst the armour plate at its thickest was approximately the same as that of the *Scharnhorst*, it covered the *Bismarck* far more extensively. The heavy guns and their installations were excellent as were the optics that directed them. These ships were very fast for their size whilst the comprehensive internal subdivision of their hulls made them very difficult to sink.

The *Bismarck* was launched with great fanfare and publicity. The whole of the Nazi government led by Hitler was in attendance, whilst the propaganda machinery was cranked into high gear in order to announce that the German navy would soon commission the most powerful warship in the world. After a largely trouble-free period of trails in the Baltic, the *Bismarck* was commissioned into the German navy in the spring of 1941. Once again Hitler was present as he had a special affection for his latest battleship in spite of being a rather poor sailor himself.

The *Bismarck* was designed as a commerce raider, the German navy having laid its plans for a war with Britain far longer then the army or even Hitler himself. To this end a string of supply ships covered the whole of the Atlantic Ocean, and elaborate codes and reconnaissance information was delivered to the major warships which were already in position when the war started. The system worked well for the 'pocket battleships' and the *Scharnhorst* and *Gneisenau* and the early submarine 'Wolf Pack' tactics were already being employed. However, the convoy system with its battleship escorts required a more powerful response and this would take the form of operation 'Rheinübung'. This operation required the *Bismarck* to sail in concert with the heavy cruiser *Prinz Eugen*. The cruiser would attack the merchant ships whilst the *Bismarck* would deal with battleship escorts.

In May 1941 the *Bismarck* and *Prinz Eugen* secretly set sail for Norway and the north Atlantic. The British knew what the Bismarck was designed for, they readily appreciated her power and the danger she represented to their life line to north America, and now they were to discover just how powerful and deadly a battleship the *Bismarck* really was.

K.M. *Bismarck*, oil on canvas, 29 x 31 inches

I.J.N. *CHIKUMA* 1939 Japanese heavy cruiser

Sister ship: *Tone*

Displacement	15,239 tons full load
Length.	661 ft
Speed.	35 knots
Complement.	874.
Guns.	8 - 8", 8 - 5", 21 - 1"
Torpedoes.	16 - 24", 8 reloads
Aircraft	6
Armour.	3.9" hull belt, 2.5" deck, 5" conning tower

The ultimate and some consider the best of the Japanese heavy cruisers, *Chikuma* and *Tone* were designed and built as scouting cruisers. The main 'eyes' of this type of ship was the float plane and this element of these ships was as important as their guns and torpedoes. The only other nation to specifically design a seaplane cruiser was Sweden with their Gotland class. With the vastness of the Pacific Ocean as their operating theatre, the *Chikuma* and her sister were designed to include great range, heavy guns, a large complement of torpedo tubes and a suite of 6 scouting float planes. The whole aft portion of the ships was given over to the aircraft, catapults and sundry equipment. This mean't that all the main guns were situated in four turrets forward of the bridge, giving the *Chikuma* and *Tone* a very sleek appearence. Habitability was a great improvement over previous Japanese cruisers where the creature comforts often left a lot to be desired.

It is interesting to note that one of the very first practical applications of the electro-mechanical computer was as a range calculator for use in battleships and heavy cruisers. These computers were designed to factor in the bearing, speed, distance and wind direction surrounding an enemy ship in order to bring the guns to bear as accurately and speedily as possible. Although the British and Americans perfected radar as an aid to accurate shooting, the Japanese computers as fitted to the *Chikuma* were state of the art and although they lagged behind their adversaries in the use of radar, with their turrets grouped together, these ships were efficient and accurate gunnery vessels. Computers were also used as ranging devices for the powerful 'Long Lance' torpedo suites that all Japanese cruisers carried, especially the *Chikuma* and *Tone*.

With one less turret, a larger amount of space was available for more powerful engines and these gave the *Chikuma* a speed in excess of 35 knots which made her among the fastest heavy cruisers in the world.

As the scouts for the fleet, *Chikuma* and *Tone* almost always acted in concert and throughout the war they fulfilled this role brilliantly. Both scouted ahead of the carriers that were to attack Pearl Harbor, they supported the landings on Wake island, they found H.M.S. *Cornwall*, *Devonshire* and *Hermes* in the Indian Ocean and directed the carrier-borne planes which sank these ships. They were also present at the battle of Midway and one of their planes discovered the U.S. aircraft carriers. They were also scouting round the Solomon Islands and successfully located the U.S. fleet prior to the battle of Santa Cruz. During this battle, *Chikuma* was hit by a bomb causing damage to her bridge. In spite of being wounded, the captain gave the order to jettison all the torpedoes in anticipation of another attack. When it came, a bomb hit the now empty torpedo deck. Had the captain's order not been given, *Chikuma* would have shared the fate of many Japanese cruisers when their torpedo complements exploded.

Chikuma's last voyage took place in late october 1944 when she and *Tone* formed part of the main striking force during the battle of Leyte Gulf. *Tone* was damaged early on in the operation but *Chikuma* was unscathed and off the coast of Samar island she was at the head of the Japanese line when the unprotected American light carriers of 'Taffy 3', supporting the landings, were completely taken by surprise. As the carriers sought protection behind their tiny screen of gallant destroyers, *Chikuma* lunged straight for the nearest carrier U.S.S. *Gambier Bay* and shot her to pieces. As that ship sank, her tormented sisters launched their planes against *Chikuma* and torpedoed her in her engine room. The damage was massive and the ship literally stopped in her tracks. She was dead in the water when the destroyer *Nowaki* rescued her crew as the bulk of the Japanese fleet retired to the north. As the *Nowaki* fled the sinking *Chikuma*, she in turn was attacked by aircraft. Hit by many bombs, all aboard were lost as the brave little *Nowaki,* which had stayed in the danger area on an errand of mercy, joined *Chikuma* at the bottom of the ocean.

I.J.N. *Chikuma*, acrylic on paper

H.M.S. EXETER 1932 British Cruiser

Sister ship: *York*

Displacement	8390 tons
Length	575 ft
Speed	32 knots
Complement	639
Guns	6 - 8", 4 - 4", 2 - 8 barrelled pom-poms
Torpedo tubes	6 - 21"
Aircraft	2
Armour	3" belt

H.M.S. *Exeter* and her sister *York*, the so called 'Cathedral Class' cruisers were built in conformity with the Washington Treaty displacement and armament limits. Following the heavy County class cruisers, a smaller vessel was called for in accordance with the new role of trade protection duties that these ships were designed to carry out.

The traditional role of the fleet scouting cruiser was now given over to the heavy destroyer whilst the heavier cruisers where designed to shadow enemy battleships. *Exeter* was lighter than the 'Counties' and carried two less heavy guns. However, their intended operational purpose was reflected in their higher speed of over 32 knots

THE BATTLE OF THE RIVER PLATE

With the outbreak of war in 1939 and the dispersal of the German armoured cruisers *Admiral Scheer* and *Admiral Graf Spee* into the Atlantic, H.M.S. *Exeter* under her new captain, F.S Bell R.N was ordered from her refitting in the Falkland Island to join the South American Station under the command of Commodore Henry Harwood, flying his flag in H.M.S. *Ajax* with H.M.Z.S *Achilles* in company off the River Plate, where he expected the *Graf Spee* to appear. Arriving on 12 December, Harwood gathered his ships' captains to outline his plan. Should the *Graf Spee* appear, he intended to split his squadron in two, *Ajax* and the *Achilles* to the south, with *Exeter* to the north. From these positions he intended to attack at once, forcing the German ship to divide her fire whilst under attack from both sides.

As dawn broke the next day, smoke was sighted on the horizon. *Exeter* in the van sighted the *Graf Spee* first, making straight for her at speed. At 0618am *Exeter* opened fire which was returned immediately and accurately. As Harwood had anticipated, *Graf Spee* was having to divide its fire between the two columns of British ships before concentrating on the *Exeter*. Soon B turret

nearest the bridge was wrecked and the bridge put out of action. The wounded Captain Bell took up position in the rear conning tower. All the communication equipment on the *Exeter* was destroyed so his orders to the remaining guns, the engine room and the sailors manually steering the ship had to be passed along lines of messengers. Then the remaining forward turret was put out of action, and all power was lost to the remaining turret aft. *Exeter* was ablaze and in serious trouble, she had been struck seven times with heavy calibre shells and damaged by numerous near misses. At this point with *Graf Spee* seemingly moving in for the kill, Commodore Harwood rapidly closed on the German ship to take the pressure off the crippled *Exeter* which was desperately trying to pull out of range under a smoke screen.

Once again *Graf Spee* was forced to turn its attention to *Ajax* and *Achilles*. The tenacity displayed by the British with their inferior forces must have had an effect on *Graf Spee*'s Captain, Hans Langsdorff. His ship had not escaped damage, with 39 of his sailors dead and many wounded, and even now the severely damaged *Exeter* was preparing to ram the German ship. All this must

H.M.S. *Exeter* opens fire on the Graf Spee at the Battle of the River Plate. (Collection of Dan S. Somekh)

have played a part in Langsdorff's subsequent decision to break off the action and make for the port of Montevideo.

Captain Bell was ordered to take the *Exeter* to the Falklands whilst the remainder of Harwood's squadron followed the *Graf Spee* into the River Plate whilst calling for reinforcements. The naval action off the River Plate was over, now the battle would be fought in the diplomatic sphere between the British and the Germans, with the Uruguayans holding the ring between them. Added to this a clever British plan of misinformation was launched to further confuse

Langsdorff and convince him that a whole fleet of Royal Navy warships were waiting to destroy him when he left Montevideo .

Unable to face further losses to his crew, Captain Langsdorff left all but a few of his men on the shore, withdrew to the outer harbour and blew his ship up. Taking sole responsibility for the action and the final destruction of his ship, Langsdorff retreated to his hotel room, wrapped himself in his ship's flag and shot himself. When H.M.S. *Exeter* returned to Plymouth in February 1940 she was met by a huge mass of people, including Winston Churchill, cheering their hero ship home.

The ship's company along with those of *Ajax* paraded through the streets of London before medals were awarded by the King and a banquet at the Guildhall was enjoyed by all. In an uncertain time, the Battle of the River Plate was a real tonic and the men of the *Exeter* were in the thick of it. They certainly deserved a better fate than that which was to befall them and their ship within two years.

Exeter was repaired and modernised before being sent to the Far East in order to deter the Japanese. Following the outbreak of the Pacific war, *Exeter* joined Admiral Doorman's mixed squadron of cruisers and destroyers in an attempt to prevent Japanese convoys from attacking the Dutch East Indies. During the extended battle of the Java Sea, Doorman's fleet faced a formidable force of enemy heavy cruisers and destroyers and during the course of the action *Exeter* was once again severely damaged and had to retire to the port of Surabaya whilst the rest of Admiral Doorman's ships were picked off one by one and sunk. Pausing only to repair her damaged engines and to bury her dead, *Exeter* and two destroyers attempted the passage to Colombo in Ceylon but did not get very far before being intercepted by more Japanese heavy cruisers and taken under a terrible fire. Virtually shelled to pieces, her captain ordered her abandoned and scuttled. Her crew had fought to the end with great bravery only to be rescued by the Japanese and finally driven into the horrors of captivity.

R.F. *STRASBOURG* 1937 French battleship

Sister ship: *Dunkerque*

Displacement	25,925 tons
Length	703 ft
Speed	29.5 knots
Complement	1,431
Guns	8 - 13", 16 - 5.1", 8 - 37mm, 32 - 0.52"
Armour	9.5" belt, 5 - 4" deck
Aircraft	3 - 4

Strasbourg and *Dunkerque* were the first French battleships constructed following the First World War. Although they had been developing plans for such ships in the 1920s, the arrival of the new concept 'pocket battleships' from Germany, and rumours of Italian construction, encouraged the French to finalise the designs of two new ships and start their building in the early 30s. The results were radical, the main armament grouped together in two massive quadruple turrets mounting brand new 13" guns, somewhat similar to the British *Nelson* and *Rodney*. A massive tower bridge mounted three linked

The French battleship *Strasbourg* escapes the British shelling of Mers el Kébir in 1940. (Collection of Dan S. Somekh)

rotating range finders weighing a total of 86 tons. Towards the rear of the ship, was a hanger and workshops for 3 or 4 flying boats. Although not as heavily armoured as some of their contemporaries, the *Strasbourg*'s speed at nearly 30 knots, was amongst the fastest. Whereas the *Rodney* and *Nelson* with their similar layout were symphonies of ugliness, the *Strasbourg* was stunningly beautiful, perfectly balanced and proportioned, they looked magnificent from every angle and seemed to have been designed with an artist's eye.

When the *Dunkerque* represented her country at the 1937 Coronation Naval Review, she created a sensation in spite of sharing that particular stage with the modern *Graf Spee* and the Japanese heavy cruiser *Ashigara*.

Sadly, the Strasbourg types were destined to play tragic roles following the sudden collapse of their country's fortunes in 1940. Following their armistice with the Germans, the new French government stated that they would not hand over their fleet to the Axis powers, but to the hard-pressed British this position represented too many uncertain and dangerous ambiguities and these had to be resolved even by force if necessary.

A large part of the French fleet was moored at their North African base in Mers el Kébir, including several battleships, the *Strasbourg* and *Dunkerque* among them, when the British battlefleet, Force H, comprising the battleships *Hood*, *Resolution* and *Valiant* and the aircraft carrier, *Ark Royal*, several cruisers and destroyers appeared on the horizon under the command of Vice-Admiral Sir James Somerville. His orders were to deliver an ultimatum to the French commander, Admiral Gensoul: 1. Sail with Force H. and continue the fight against the Germans and the Italians. 2. Sail to a British port and be disarmed. 3. Sail to a French possession in the West Indies. 4. Scuttle your ships within 6 hours. If none of these conditions were met, the British would destroy the French ships with gunfire.

It is difficult to know what went through the French Admiral's mind at this desperate moment, but as he had recently commanded an Anglo-French squadron which had included H.M.S. *Hood*, Somerville's flagship, perhaps his haughty manner was understandable if not advisable under the circumstances he found himself in. Gensoul decided to play for time whilst secretly calling on France to send reinforcements and raising steam in his own ships. These messages were intercepted by the British and the Admiralty signalled to Somerville to force the issue without delay. By the late afternoon, it was obvious that the French were in no mood to listen so at 5.54pm the British battlefleet opened fire.

The resulting slaughter and destruction was terrible, one battleship had blown up, another was sinking, a destroyer had its stern blown clean off and Gensoul's flagship *Dunkerque* was severely damaged. Only the *Strasbourg* and four destroyers managed to raise steam and bravely escape the inferno. Chased by the *Hood* and harried by *Ark Royal*'s aircraft the sad little flotilla made it back to Toulon in Southern France.

Dunkerque was repaired and rejoined *Strasbourg* at the naval base in Toulon and there sat with other considerable units of the French fleet in idleness and despair, without a friend, their neutral existence entirely dependent on the Germans. And it was the Germans who, as the British had predicted, eventually swept the Vichy government aside and sought to capture the French fleet. This time the French commander had anticipated the German betrayal and on 27 November 1942, as the Nazi troops entered the town, he gave the command to blow up the entire fleet. In the greatest act of naval self-destruction in all history, 87 warships were sunk at their moorings, the gallant *Strasbourg* amongst them.

I.J.N. *YAMATO* 1941 Japanese Battleship

Sister ship: *Musashi.*

Displacement	71,659 tons full load
Length	862 ft
speed	27 knots
Complement	2,500
Guns	9 - 18.1", 6 - 6.1", 12 - 5". 150 - 25mm
Armour	16.1" hull belt. 9" deck, 25" turrets
Aircraft	7

By 1934, the Japanese were set on a course to expand their empire into China and into the South Seas. Her naval planners fully realised that such moves were unlikely to go unchallenged by the U.S. Navy. Japan's naval constructors had already proved themselves to be innovators in the design of heavy cruisers, destroyers and aircraft carriers. However, as far as modern battleship construction was concerned, Japan was bound by the international treaty obligations which restricted the building of such ships unless they were to replace existing units and were not to exceed 35,000 tons. In the light of her her territorial ambitions, Japan decided to break the treaties in spirit and in fact.

The Japanese calculated that in a war with America, she could never hope to outbuild the U.S. shipyards. Therefore she would embark on a stategy of building a few battleships of such a size and power that they would be able to defeat any fleet ranged against them. They also calculated that any U.S. battleships of comparable size would not be able to pass through the locks of the Panama Canal.

In order to maintain a charade of international co-operation, the planning, construction, and commissioning of such ships would have to be carried out in the utmost secrecy, even to the Japanese people themselves. The design of the new 'super' ships was entrusted to the master naval architects Keiji Fukuda and Yuzuru Hiraga. No one had contemplated warships of such a massive scale and, before the final plans were completed, no less than 23 different designs were formulated. Hundreds of design problems had to be overcome, theories tried and discarded, many hull designs were tested in special tanks, massive guns had to be designed and tested and tons of special armour plate had to be rolled and milled. To build a warship that was all but unsinkable, virtually impregnable and more powerful than anything seen before was a stupendous

undertaking, especially for a country like Japan with a shaky economy and little or no natural resources. Four ships were laid down but only two were completed as battleships. They were given the names *Yamato* and *Musashi*, *Yamato* being the ancient spiritual name of Japan itself . Whilst this ship was constructed in the secure naval dockyard in Kure, the *Musashi* was built in the commercial dockyards of Nagasaki where security could be compromised. In order to keep prying eyes away from the huge construction project, the whole public area surrounding the dockyard was demolished and a huge warehouse was constructed in front of the yard. The yard itself was covered with a giant curtain of sisal rope and the dockyard workers and ship designers were watched round the clock by the secret police. There were several cases of unlucky workers who bragged about their work in local bars only to mysteriously 'disappear', never to be seen or heard from again.

In spite of such measures, word did get out concerning the construction of new, secret battleships and other nations were becoming concerned. In reply to questions concerning warships with 16" guns, the Japanese, somewhat disingenuously stated that they were not building battleships with 16" guns.

In fact the Yamato and her sister mounted 18.1" armament, the greatest ever carried in a warship before or since. They represented a quantum leap in naval artillery, firing a shell the weight of a large car. The armour plate was the thickest and most comprehensive for ships of their size and the complex subdivision of their internal spaces were designed to make *Yamato* and *Musashi* virtually unsinkable. A huge bulbous extension was added to the base of their bows in order to streamline their passage through the water (all ships have this feature now). Every part of the *Yamato* was built on a heroic scale, armour covered every part of the ship above the decks to protect the crews from the

concussion of her main guns, even the lifeboats and the seven aircraft she carried were housed internally. At 71,659 tons full load, *Yamato* was 25 per cent heavier than the German *Bismarck* and dwarfed the contemporary British battleships. Their huge optical range finders mounted atop streamlined tower bridges were state of the art and gave the *Yamato* and her sister a range of gunfire of at least 37,000 yards. Only in their speed of 27 knots were they slower then their contemporaries, and in the important field of radar the Japanese were far behind their British and American rivals. By all accounts nothing had been spared in the quality of their construction and when they were completed, with their undulating decks (a Hiraga trade mark) to give the huge hull extra strength, they presented a beauty of line and form allied to massive power that has seldom been equalled in a warship.

Inspite of this, the *Yamato* and her sister were not commissioned without a lot of debate within Japanese naval circles. The Commander in Chief, Admiral Yamamoto, had pioneered naval aviation to a high degree, as he was to prove at Pearl Harbor and off the coast of Malaya when his aviators showed just how vulnerable battleships were to determined aircraft attack. He considered the new 'super' ships to be no more than useless, outdated 'paper tigers'. In his poetic phrase, "The greatest serpent can be destroyed by a swarm of bees!", Yamamoto was to be proved correct.

Throughout the war, the *Yamato* and *Musashi* were seldom employed aggressively. It was as if the Japanese feared that if their giant creations were to be lost then something of the spirit of Japan would be lost as well. Tactically, naval warfare was now the war of the aircraft carrier, with battleships in support of their operations, hardly the scenario that the *Yamato* was designed for. Only when the Americans attacked the Philippines in late 1944 was the whole Japanese navy called upon to defeat the landings. In the huge battle of Leyte Gulf that followed, the main Japanese fleet set out to destroy the American transports and landing craft. Not long into their voyage, the Japanese lost the 'unsinkable' *Musashi* to a veritable hailstorm of torpedoes and bombs. However, the fleet pressed on and much to the surprise of the Japanese and the shock of the Americans, the *Yamato* and her squadron caught the undefended transports and their light carrier escorts off the coast of Samar Island. At this

moment, the *Yamato*'s huge guns roared into life in anger for the first time in the war. In a confused, and on the American part, a heroic David and Goliath defending action, the Japanese sank one small escort carrier and three destroyers whist receiving severe damage to themselves before retiring from the battle.

From this point, the Japanese navy had lost control of the war, the *Yamato* and a small fleet of destroyers and cruisers were all that were left to Japan when the invasion of Okinawa began in April, 1945. In a last desperate gamble, the *Yamato* was ordered south to defend the islands. Halfway to her destination, *Yamato* was spotted and attacked by over 350 planes, as many as the Japanese had used themselves in the Pearl Harbor attack. To the Americans, the *Yamato* represented the last vestige of Japanese naval power and they were determined upon her destruction. In a furious series of attacks, the mighty *Yamato* received at least 10 bomb hits and twelve torpedoes before capsizing and blowing up in a shattering explosion.

With this battle, the Imperial Japanese Navy ceased to exist and the lost *Yamato* passed into legend in Japan. A special museum housing a huge model *Yamato* is dedicated to her memory in Kure, the place of her birth. Countless books, movies and even an animated 'Spaceship Yamato', mysteriously raised from the bottom of the oceans to do battle in the galaxies, keep the legend alive. More pages of the internet are devoted to this vessel than any other battleship and imagined battles between *Yamato* and her contemporaries are fought over cyberspace. Although her war service was limited, the battleship *Yamato* still inspires interest throughout the world and engenders immense pride in the country of her origin as the greatest armoured warship ever to sail the seas.

I.J.N. *Yamato*, acrylic on paper, 18 x 25 inches

THE U-BOAT CAMPAIGN 1939-45

In 1919 the Treaty of Versailles expressly forbade Germany to construct and commission submarines. The U-boat arm of the German Navy had nearly cost Britain the war and although the menace was finally defeated by the convoy system, it was a close run thing. However, the remnants of the German Navy secretly had no intention of falling behind in the latest submarine technology. They set up a front organisation in Holland under the name Ingenier-Kantoor voor Scheepsbouw to design and supervise the building of modern submarines, utilising the latest thinking and technological skills to be put at the service of Germany when she would rise again. The mastermind behind this deception was none other then the armaments king Gustav von Krupp and it would be his shipyards that started building the first U-boats in Germany twelve years later.

When Hitler came to power in 1933 and German rearmament began, the head of the intended U-boat fleet was a certain Karl Doenitz, who had served in submarines in the First World War and had been captured by the British. Whilst in prison camp, Doenitz pondered on U-boat tactics for any future war. When he became head of the U-boat arm, he formulated and developed his theories of attacks on convoys en masse, the so-called ' Wolf Pack' tactic which involved convoys being attacked by upwards of 20 U-boats at a time, using single scouts to locate and track a convoy whilst calling up the 'Wolf Pack' to bear down on the merchant ships and destroy them in co-ordinated attacks.

In order to achieve success, Doenitz calculated he would need at least 200 U-boats for a prolonged campaign. To make these plans a reality, he would have to convince the C in C of the German Navy Erich Raeder and Adolf Hitler. Admiral Raeder had already had his' Z plan' approved which involved a massive expansion of the German surface fleet to challenge British sea power. However, this fleet would not be ready until at least 1944–45. Hitler, who had at best, a sketchy knowledge of sea power and its uses, saw battleships as dramatic symbols of power and political leverage. Neither he or Raeder were convinced that a nation like Germany should give up its battleships and concentrate on submarine warfare. Yet, on every level, Doenitz was to be proved correct, not least on the economic front. It cost Germany 4,000,000 Reichmarks apiece to build the *Bismarck* and *Tirpitz*, whereas such an outlay would have built 100 U-boats.

When war broke out five years ahead of Admiral Raeder's schedule, Germany had 57 U-boats in commission with highly trained crews. The Germans adhered strictly to the International rules governing submarine warfare. Although somewhat impractical, these laws laid down that all merchant ships were to be stopped and their crews and passengers were allowed to leave in the lifeboats before the ship was either taken as a prize or sunk by gunfire. Only warships and troopships were to be sunk on sight.

Even these rules were not infallible as when very early on in the war, the liner SS. *Athenia* on passage to New York was torpedoed having been mistaken for a troopship. Not withstanding these restrictions, the highly professional captains and crews scored some notable successes. The aircraft carrier *Courageous* was torpedoed and sunk in the Channel approaches on 17 September, and shortly after this possibly the most audacious submarine attack of the whole war took place in the Home Fleet base at Scapa Flow when Gunther Prien, commander of U.47, penetrated the base defences and torpedoed the battleship *Royal Oak* which sank with a great loss of life. More success might have come but for the fact, initially, that the Germans were using faulty torpedoes which sometimes failed to explode when they hit a target.

In August, 1940, Hitler declared a total blockade of the British Isles. This meant that the U-boat rules no longer applied and any ship could be sunk without warning. The Battle of the Atlantic had begun. The 'Wolf Packs' went into action and the shipping losses began to rise dramatically. By the end of the summer 58 ships totalling 284,000 tons had been lost, and in the month of October alone a further 63 totalling 352,000 tons were sent to the bottom. Like fighter pilots, several U-boat commanders became 'aces'; Lt. Commander Schultze of U.48 became the first U-boat captain to achieve a score of 100,000 tons of shipping, but not long after this the indefatigable Prien racked up a score of 200,000 tons. These 'aces' were followed by such U-boat luminaries as Joachim Schepke and Otto Kretschmer who became like film stars in Germany, nothing was too good for these men and their crews. Special 'sun' hotels were reserved for them in the German Alps and all of them were bedecked with honours and medals from a grateful nation.

By 1941, the losses of merchant shipping was greater than could be replaced, forcing Churchill to issue his 'Battle of the Atlantic' order which gave priority to the defeat of the U-boat menace. But U-boat warfare was increasingly becoming a dangerous business not only for the merchant marine but also for their attackers. In the month of March two 'aces' Prien and Schepke were lost and Otto Kretschmer was captured. The so called 'Happy Time' for the U-boats was over, but still more U-boats were coming on stream, over two hundred had been commissioned and whilst 47 had been lost, the wind was still with the U-boats.

When the Americans entered the war, they chose to ignore the advice given to them over the convoy system by the British and had to learn the lessons of 1917 all over again at a fearful cost when Doenitz switched his 'Wolf Packs' to the Eastern Seaboard and the waters of Central and South America. Unprotected tankers and other merchant ships sailed the seas in peacetime order, usually singly, without escorts and lights ablaze and incessant radio traffic drawing the 'Wolf Packs' to them. The resulting slaughter was

Coastal Command Liberator attacking a U-boat, acrylic on board, 13 x 19 inches

horrendous. In the second 'Happy Time', the U-boats dispatched 327,000 tons of American shipping to the bottom in December 1941 to January 1942.

When the U.S. navy belatedly instituted a convoy system, Doenitz once again switched his submarines to the mid Atlantic and destroyed 3,000,000 tons of allied shipping in the first six months of 1943. By this time, Hitler had lost faith in his surface fleet, banishing them to northern Norway as a 'fleet in being'. The demoralised Raeder resigned and Doenitz became his successor. From now on, the entire German naval effort would be placed behind the U-boats. Ironically at this time in mid 1943, the U-boat menace was suddenly checked. Advanced escort tactics, new depth charge weapons and long-range radar-equipped Liberator aircraft began to master the U-boats and, although the sinkings of merchant shipping continued, the U-boat hunters became the hunted. The U-boats were simply overwhelmed by the allied defences and superior technology and, although new advanced submarines had been designed, they were not yet ready to make good the losses the U-boats were increasingly suffering. By the time these new boats could have made a difference, Germany

had lost the war. Admiral Doenitz had one more duty to perform. As Hitler's designated successor, he had to supervise the unconditional surrender of all the German forces including the 200 U-boats left to the German navy. His gallant crews had nearly succeeded in strangling the Atlantic lifeline that kept Britain in the war, but this must be weighed in the balance with the loss of 650 U-boats and 30,000 of their personnel. Countless allied seamen died in the longest costliest and most deadly naval battle of all time.

A strange postscript to this story occurred at the Nuremberg trials where Karl Doenitz stood on trial for his life. He was accused of unrestricted and inhuman submarine warfare. His defence team called as a star witness, non other that Admiral Chester Nimitz the C in C of the American Pacific Fleet. Nimitz readily admitted by letter, that in destroying the Japanese merchant marine and a large part of the Japanese navy, he had employed the same submarine 'Wolf Pack' tactics that he had learned from the Germans. The Nuremberg court accepted Nimitz's testimony and Doenitz was sentenced to prison for 20 years.

BRITISH SUBMARINES IN WORLD WAR II

Following their experiences with the so called ' Fleet Submarines' of the First World War, the British had a few more tries at this impractical idea. The extraordinary M Class were as big as their steam-driven cousins and, although conventionally powered, they carried a huge 12" battleship gun which could fire above and below the water. As an added bonus, they removed one of these guns and substituted a small airplane, the Parnell Peto, and a hanger to service and launch it from.

Unfortunately the spirit of carelessness that hung over the steam submarines also attended this aircraft carrier when the vessel crashed dived, someone had forgotten to close the hanger door, and the submarine became inundated and sank to the bottom taking all her crew with her.

Undaunted by these British failures, the Americans developed their own version of the fleet submarine, the *Argonaut*, a Jules Verne contraption which, like its British cousins was a total failure. The French had a go with the *Surcouf*, a massive boat which tried to combine big guns (two 8") and aircraft. *Surcouf* was too big for its own good, a bad sea boat and during its short service, a nearly mutinous crew. She was lost in the Caribbean in collision with a freighter.

But the last word must go to the Japanese, the builders of the greatest battleship set about building the biggest submarines, the stupendous I 400 class. These monsters weighed in at 3,530 tons, as big as a light cruiser. Their mission was to bomb the Panama Canal and to this end, they carried three purpose-built aircraft and parts for a fourth, all contained in a large hanger with a set of rails running half the length of the ship in order to blast the aircraft off on their mission. The war ended even as these huge submarines were on their way to their targets.

Only the Germans seemed to understand the true purpose of the submarine, and it was not an underwater battleship or an aircraft carrier but a silent commerce killer. Having all but destroyed Britain's lifelines in the Great War, she now prepared secretly for the next conflict with new efficient boats, the 'Atlantik' V class, the most numerous type of submarine ever built, and using the 'Wolf Pack' system of massed attacks they nearly succeeded for a second time.

The Royal Navy knew that they would never be called upon to attack convoys on this scale, their submarines would fulfil many different roles, scouting, attacking warships and supply ships and landing agents on enemy shores. The British boats would attack singly, always with great daring and skill, certainly no less heroically then the German or American submarine crews, yet in the minds of the public at large the 'Silent Service' remained just that. Only two feature films figured British submarine exploits and both of them starred John Mills. Compared to Hollywood and latterly Germany whose studio submarines forever seemed to be diving into danger, the exploits of the 'Perishers' (the British name for submariners), went almost unnoticed in the public's imagination. The real story of the Royal Navy's submarine service deserves much more exposure. They sent over 2 million tons of enemy shipping to the bottom including 78 warships. 270 British submarines were commissioned into the Royal Navy and 78 were lost. Three submarine commanders were awarded Victoria Crosses, Malcolm Wanklyn in *Upholder*, Tony Miers in *Torbay*, and 'Tubby' Linton in *Turbulent*. Lt. Commander Wanklyn was part of the 10th submarine flotilla operating out of Malta and was responsible for sinking 3 U-boats, one destroyer and 19 supply ships before he and his crew were lost on 14 April 1942.

One famous visitor to our shores during the Coronation Review in 1937, the Japanese heavy cruiser *Ashigara*, met her end at the hands of Lt. Commander 'Baldy' Hezlets in the submarine H.M.S. *Trenchant* when he put 5 torpedoes into her whilst the Japanese ship was underway in the Banka Straight.

The 'Silent Service prosecuted their war with vigour, expertise and tremendous courage and 3,142 brave 'Perishers' paid the price. Without them, the war in North Africa could not have been won, without them many gallant men and women who secretly served their countries against the Nazis would not have been able to operate, let alone survive. Without them the mighty battleship *Tirpitz* would have been a far greater menace than she actually was. The British submariners do not need oceans of celluloid to tell their story, their deeds speak for themselves.

British S class submarine on patrol, bookjacket illustration for *Not Thinking of Death*, Alexander Fullerton (Little Brown)

THE END OF H.M.S. *HOOD*

World War Two came before the navies of the combatants were ready. The German navy was caught with its two new battleships, *Bismarck* and *Tirpitz* still fitting out in the dockyards, whilst the head of the Reich's navy, Admiral Erich Reader, who had planned for a war with Britain in 1944 when his projected fleet would have been ready, was left with a barely adequate force only one-third of its planned wartime strength.

As for the Royal Navy, her newest battleships, the King George V class were still being built, some needing two more years in the builder's yards. The modernisation of the existing battleships and cruisers was not yet complete and in the case of Britain's most famous warship, H.M.S. *Hood,* it had not even been started. And this modernisation was long overdue. Her secondary armament was antiquated, her fire control systems needed updating, her engines needed overhauling and most of all she needed more armour plating over her vulnerable decks. Had the *Hood* been modernised, her stately appearance would have been radically changed, more businesslike, more like a modern man-of-war, more fit for the purpose of modern naval warfare. But her original grace and beauty would have gone. Like the ageing film star whose looks we fondly remember in their bloom, H.M.S. *Hood* would enter the war, still beautiful, still powerful, but ageing rapidly.

Her first operations were convoy protection and hunting for enemy raiders with the ships of her French allies. Within the 6 weeks of May-June 1940, this ally would collapse and *Hood* was despatched with force H under the command of Vice Admiral Sir James Somerville to the French naval base of Mers el Kébir in order to try and induce the French Fleet to join him or accept destruction. Perhaps understandably, the French commander refused to accept the ultimatum and the reluctant British opened fire on the crowded anchorage.

The resulting destruction and slaughter was terrible and for many years the French would find it difficult to forgive their erstwhile ally, but in the brutal world of politics and war, a point had to be made, Britain had been forced into war and thus fully committed, no one was to be left in any doubt that she would fight to the bitter end, what ever the cost. This point was not lost upon the Germans or more particularly on the neutral United States with its appeasers and isolationists who doubted whether the British had the will or the means to fight.

H.M.S. *Hood* went into dry dock to have her 5" guns removed to be replaced by 4" anti-aircraft guns and a perfectly useless and dangerous weapon called the Unrotated Projectile Launcher or U.P. for short. This fantastic nonsense consisted of a box of rockets which, when fired in the direction of enemy aircraft, would open a parachute and drift down with a bomb suspended from this parachute, inviting the Nazi bombers to obligingly fly into the barrage. These 'wonder weapons' were scattered all over the boat deck of the *Hood.*

The spring of 1941 found the *Hood* based at Scapa Flow as part of the Home Fleet where on 22 May, signals were received that the new German Battleship *Bismarck* and the heavy cruiser *Prinz Eugen* had left their anchorage in Norway and disappeared into the North Atlantic. The C in C of the Home Fleet, Admiral Sir John Tovey immediately dispatched the *Hood* and the new battleship *Prince of Wales*, to cover the southern tip of the Denmark Strait off the coast of Iceland should the German ships break out into the Mid Atlantic and threaten the vital convoy routes. This battle squadron was commanded by Admiral Sir Lancelot Holland, one of the most popular and respected officers in the Royal Navy. Due to the bad weather, the *Bismarck* and her consort had been effectively lost but on 23 May the cruisers *Suffolk* and *Norfolk* patrolling the Denmark strait spotted them heading south. Their position was radioed to Holland who anticipated that if they maintained their course, battle would be joined at dawn the next day.

As the British ships raced through the night, the preparation for action stations were made. A clean set of clothing was put on, letters written in the hope that they would never be sent, and early meals were taken to fortify the men against the bitter cold of the ceaseless watches. As dawn came up on 24 May, 'Empire Day', the signal was flashed from the *Prince of Wales* to H.M.S. *Hood* and the Admiralty - "Enemy in sight !"

The British and German ships were shaping an almost parallel course with the British slightly ahead. However, Admiral Holland desired that the range be closed to protect his weak decks from long range plunging fire. This meant that for a few minutes only the forward guns would be available to the British. H.M.S. *Hood* opened fire first, after mistaking the *Prinz Eugen* in the lead of the German line, for the *Bismarck*, the principal target . The *Bismarck* followed shortly after, targeting the *Hood*. The opening salvoes from the *Hood* were finding the range but so were the *Bismarck*'s shells and those of the *Prinz Eugen*, one of which smashed into *Hood*'s boat deck amidst the rockets for the useless U.P. weapons. These rockets started to whiz around all over the boat deck starting a huge fire. Those watching the flagship from the *Prince of Wales* were concerned about the fire but were also thrilled by the sight of the wonderful old ship charging through the seas at full power, her huge battle ensigns flying and turning to bring all her guns to bear on the enemy. Then the fifth salvo from the *Bismarck* arrived.

Empire Day, 1941, commissioned by Ron Feltham. Donated by Ron Feltham to The Royal Navy Museum, Portsmouth

Three shell splashes were spotted falling around the *Hood* but the forth shell penetrated the boat deck just forward of the main mast, plunging into the 4" ammunition and in turn touching off the main magazines serving the two rear turrets.

The resulting explosion tore the great ship apart, everything aft of the foremast, turrets, guns, masts, boats was blown into the sky whilst the fore part of the ship reared vertically into the air before slipping back into the sea. Within 90 seconds, H.M.S. *Hood* had literally disappeared. Only a huge cloud of smoke marked her passage into history.

The nature of naval warfare is both magnificent and terrible. The 'Mighty *Hood*' had steamed into action at full speed, with flags flying and guns blazing, to her destruction. At one moment she was there in all her magnificent glory, then in the blink of an eye, she was gone, but this beautiful warship was more than just steel and grace, she was above all the 1421 brave young men eager to do their expected duty but fearful that that duty may involve the ultimate sacrifice. Honour and glory has a price and sometimes that price is too terrible even to imagine. On H.M.S. *Hood*, on the day of her death, 1418 men including their admiral, paid that price.

THE END OF THE BATTLESHIP *BISMARCK*

Operation 'Rheinübung', the mission of the German battleship *Bismarck* and the heavy cruiser *Prinz Eugen*, to break out into the mid Atlantic and prey on the vital allied convoy routes, was planned by Admiral Raeder, the head of the German navy as a bid to prove the value of the German surface fleet in the face of Royal Navy superiority. This mission was entrusted to the experienced Vice-Admiral Gunter Lutjens, recently returned with the battleships *Scharnhorst* and *Gneisenau* from a successful raiding cruise.

However, both these ships were undergoing urgent repairs and the *Bismarck*'s sistership *Tirpitz* had not yet completed her trails, so the mission would only be undertaken by two ships. Both Hitler and Lutjens expressed doubts concerning the mission, preferring to wait until more units could be employed but they were persuaded by Raeder whose rationale for the mission was that the Royal Navy was stretched both in the Mediterranean and the Atlantic and would not be able to hunt the *Bismarck* and *Prinz Eugen* effectively. Raeder also had another agenda, the head of the submarine arm of the German Navy, Karl Doenitz, was pressing for more U-boat construction at the expense of the surface fleet and Raeder felt that the traditional navy had something to prove.

The sinking of H.M.S. *Hood* so early into the mission, seemed to vindicate Raeder's decision and the forcing of the *Prince of Wales* to retire under fire from the action only underlined his determination to commit his triumphant ships into the Atlantic. But what he failed to realise was that the mission was already over. Although the *Prince of Wales* had been badly damage, she had hit back and *Bismarck* was now losing precious fuel oil from a ruptured tank in the forward part of the ship. Lutjens realised that if the operation stood any chance of success, he would have to put into St Nazaire on the French coast in order to carry out repairs. With this in mind, he released the *Prinz Eugen* to the south to act alone as a commerce raider whilst the *Bismarck* headed east for France. In order to do this he had to shake off his pursuers, *Norfolk* and *Suffolk* who were still shadowing him. This he eventually managed and from 25 May, the *Bismarck* was missing somewhere in the mid Atlantic.

In Britain the sudden loss of H.M.S. *Hood* was a devastating shock. If people knew next to nothing of the Royal Navy, they did at least know that in H.M.S. *Hood* they possessed the biggest warship in the world and now she was gone with a terrible loss of life, it was something like the death of an old and dear friend. Winston Churchill as usual, caught the public mood when he issued his terse command to Admiral Tovey aboard his flagship - "Sink the *Bismarck*! ". In order to achieve this, all the resources available to the Royal Navy would have to be employed from all points of the compass to converge on the mid

Atlantic in search of their elusive quarry. The ships now ranged against the *Bismarck* included at least 4 battleships, 2 aircraft carriers, 10 cruisers and numerous destroyers. But where was the *Bismarck*?

Inexplicably, Lutjens broke radio silence to transmit a long message to Hitler and the German naval headquarters describing the recent action. The British picked up this message and after a while a Catalina flying boat spotted the *Bismarck*. Air attacks were immediately launched from H.M.S. *Ark Royal* and although the met with little success, they knew where the ship was heading and more attacks were on the way.

Admiral Lutjens addressed the crew of the *Bismarck* in order to thank them for their good wishes on his birthday and to congratulate them on the destruction of the *Hood*. Lutjens who was by no means the lightest of speakers or the most spontaneous of men, then proceeded to outline the coming odds against their safe return. The crew's morale, so lately heightened by their success, plummeted.

Meanwhile, another swordfish attack was coming in, only this time they attacked the shadowing H.M.S. *Sheffield* in mistake for the *Bismarck*. The light was failing and the *Bismarck* was making good progress to her destination, whilst Sir John Tovey and his fleet of two battleships and several cruisers and destroyers was at least 100 miles to the north. Urgent messages were sent to the *Ark Royal* to slow the enemy down at all costs.

The last possible attack flight was making its way to the *Bismarck* and was soon met with a hail of anti-aircraft fire. But, by a miracle, two torpedoes struck home, one striking the armour plate causing little damage, the other struck the rudders jamming them to port. This hit was to prove fatal. The ship was no longer in effective control and her steering gear could not be repaired in spite of heroic efforts by her crew. She now began to describe a wide circle to the north, straight into the path of the oncoming British, steaming at best speed to intercept her.

In spite of words of encouragement from Hitler himself, the mood on the *Bismarck* continued to collapse as her unhappy sailors, including their gloomy Admiral, contemplated their coming doom.

At 8.15 on the morning of 27th May, like actors in a play whose ending was already known, the British fleet appeared and the last act of the drama began. Admiral Tovey with his flag in the Battleship *King George V* in concert with the older but more powerful battleship, *Rodney*, arranged his dispositions and at 8.47 opened fire.

The *Bismarck*'s opening salvoes found *Rodney*'s range but the old ship hit back with devastatingly accurate fire, blasting the *Bismarck*'s command centre

to pieces and probably killing all the senior personnel including Admiral Lutjens and depriving the ship of any sort of central command. From this point, each of the *Bismarck*'s huge turrets was methodically smashed until all her guns fell silent. By this time, H.M.S. *Rodney* had closed to point blank range and was relentlessly firing full broadsides into the *Bismarck*.

The carnage above the decks was indescribable but the German ship would not sink, a testament to the toughness of her design. Debate has raged from that day to this as to who sank the *Bismarck*, was it H.M.S. *Dorsetshire* who fired three torpedoes into the ship or was it the crew who were ordered to scuttle her. It was probably both causes that caused the battleship *Bismarck* to capsize and sink at 10.36. Out of a complement of 2,200 men, only 118 were saved.

In response to Churchill's terse signal, the Admiralty received the equally terse reply from the Commander in Chief, Home Fleet :

'*BISMARCK* SUNK. 1036 HOURS'

THE ATLANTIC CONVOYS

The Battle of the Atlantic was the longest single military campaign of the Second World War. Starting from the first day of the European conflict and ending with the surrender of Germany in 1945, this battle involved all the elements of modern naval warfare, convoys, surface raiders, submarines, escort ships, aircraft, radar and sonar detection devices and the encryption of cyphers and codes. As Churchill recognised from the outset, the outcome of this battle would determine the course of the war, the stakes were that high. As a military struggle the loss in men and material was on a stupendous scale, 30,248 merchant and Royal Navy seamen were lost, 3,500 merchant ships were sunk, 783 U-boats and 28,000 German sailors perished along with 175 warships from both sides. Balanced against this were the millions of men, armaments and essential supplies that made it safely across the Atlantic in spite of the relentless enemy efforts to destroy their convoys.

Although the U-boats were the continuous factor throughout this battle, the opening moves belonged to the German surface raiders, *Scharnhorst, Gneisenau, Graf Spee, Admiral Scheer, Prinz Eugen* and *Bismarck*. All of these vessels were eventually checked causing Hitler to remove his remaining surface fleet to Norway to counter the expected allied invasion of that country that loomed ever larger in his mind. As a result he gave his new Naval Chief, Admiral Karl Doenitz, Germany's principal submarine strategist, carte blanche to conduct the naval war using unrestricted submarine warfare, and all future naval construction was to be given over to the production of U-boats.

In the 1930s the Royal Navy considered it had mastered any future submarine threat with the perfection of the ASDIC detection system and were thus somewhat unprepared for the new 'Wolf Pack' tactics Doenitz was developing. In the First World War U-boats operated and attacked singly and were only defeated when the convoy system was introduced. The 'Wolf Pack' was a highly controlled and concentrated form of attack on convoys, mostly under the cover of darkness with many U-boats taking part in any one operation, thus swamping the convoy escorts and rendering defence almost impossible.

The solution was to hunt down the U-boats before they were able to get among the convoys but for this to be effective the Royal Navy had to know where in the Atlantic they would be stationed. The German Naval High command was known to be using a form of 'Enigma' cypher to send coded instructions to their submarines which would be located on a secret map reference somewhere in the Atlantic. The cryptographers at Bletchley Park had broken the German army cypher but the naval version was much more difficult. On 9 May 1941, the breakthrough came when U.110 was forced to the surface and captured with her Enigma machine and grid reference tables intact.

These were handed over to the brilliant Professor Alan Turing at Bletchley Park, who not only broke the German naval codes but constructed the world's first electronic programable computer, the huge 'Colossus' which was able to read these codes as they were transmitted by the Germans to their U-boats almost as soon as the transmissions had been sent. With this priceless information and new scientific detection devices that were being developed, the British knew that the U-boat menace could be mastered. However before this could be done, further disasters in the Battle of the Atlantic would befall the allies.

When America entered the war at the end of 1941, she at least could call on the British experience to guide them in tackling the U-boat danger, that is if they were prepared to listen to advice which unfortunately they were not. The U.S. Commander in Chief Admiral Ernest King's hatred of the British bordered on mania and he would not entertain the escorted convoy system and coastal blackout measures advocated by his British allies even as Doenitz's U-boats were closing in on the eastern seaboard of his country. The resulting slaughter of these unprotected American ships was as terrible as it was predictable and avoidable; in the months from December to May 350,000 tons of American shipping and countless American sailors paid the price for this stupid man's intransigence. When the escorted convoy and blackout systems were finally adopted, the tables turned and Doenitz's eastern seaboard campaign collapsed.

The Battle of the Atlantic reached its peak of ferocity in mid 1943 when the German losses in men and U-boats suddenly became unsustainable and Doenitz had to withdraw the remaining U-boats back to their French Atlantic coast bases in order to regroup. But by then the initiative had passed to the allies and, as the huge convoys increased, the U-boat threat diminished. It was the indomitable courage of the countless merchant seamen, the Royal Navy; the Royal Canadian Navy and the U.S. Navy, the numerous scientists who provided the means to overcome the U-boats and the unsung heroes and heroines of Bletchley Park that finally defeated the Nazis on the high seas and won the Battle of the Atlantic.

Atlantic Convoy, bookjacket illustration for *The Torch Bearers*, Alexander Fullerton (Little Brown)

ESCORT CARRIERS IN THE BATTLE OF THE ATLANTIC

The escort carrier or 'Jeep' carrier (to give it its American name) was conceived, built and pressed into service in a hurry to meet the huge U-boat threat in the Atlantic at a most crucial stage in that epic battle. From the early days of the Battle of the Atlantic, convoys were threatened not only by U-boats but also from long range German aircraft. The most troublesome of these was the Focke Wulf FW 200 Kondor, a large aircraft originally built as an airliner (one of these was used as Hitler's personal transport) and converted into a large maritime bomber carrying 4,630 lbs of bombs and, late in its career, guided missiles. The Kondor posed a considerable threat to our convoys and the Royal Navy never had enough fleet and light carriers to protect them.

Two solutions were tried, one of these was the CAM (Catapult Assisted Merchant) ship. This consisted of a merchant ship with launching rails for a rocket assisted catapult for a Hurricane fighter. Once the Focke Wulf was spotted, the CAM ships launched their fighter on a one-way trip, to attack the bomber and then land in the sea. The pilot was saved (hopefully) but the aircraft was lost.

In spite of the improvised nature of the CAM ships, they were successful in blunting the Kondor attacks, but there still remained the larger problem of the U-boats. Britain, Canada and latterly the U.S. could maintain air cover up to 1000 miles from their coasts but that still left a 1000 mile 'gap' where U-boats could patrol on the surface, immune from air attacks. The British were the first to try and seal this gap with converted merchant ships with carrier decks, employing six of these. But this was not enough, so they turned to the Americans through the Lend Lease programme instituted by both governments, and the U.S. government sought the help of shipbuilder Henry Kaiser who in turn designed the systems-built ship to replaced lost tonnage in merchant shipping. This involved building all parts of the ship away from the

dockyard, numbering them and then transporting the pieces to the dockyards for final assembly. This method did not require armies of skilled shipwrights, but instead utilising semi- and non-skilled labour, assembling the ships like cars. The same method would be employed to build the small escort carriers the British required and at considerable speed.

The design was based on the U.S.S. *Bogue*, an 11,420 ton carrier built on a merchant ship hull and armed with 18 aircraft. Their names were changed (H.M.S. *Battler* is pictured here) and 34 of them were handed over to the Royal Navy.

As built, the ships carried a heavy duty laundry and a 'Gedunk' bar. This bar had slot machines for the sailors to while away their time, facilities for making ice cream, also selling cigarettes, and because the U.S. Navy has always been 'dry', coffee and soft drinks. Once these ships passed into British hands, all these 'fripperies' were done away with, no laundry, no slot machines, out with the ice cream and soft drinks, and as the Royal Navy has always been decidedly 'wet', the only luxuries allowed were booze and fags.

Armed with Avenger, Seafire and Hellcat aircraft, these escort carriers effectively closed the 'gap' and helped put the final nail into the U-boat offensive.

Meanwhile in the Pacific, these 'Jeep' carriers did sterling service in the island-hopping campaign against the Japanese, achieving immortality during the Battle of Samar when they had to defend themselves against a powerful Japanese force.

Slow, cheap and cheerful, there was many a merchant seaman who drew comfort from the presence of these so called 'Woolworth' carriers in their convoys, and their service was one of the major factors in winning the war in the Atlantic.

H.M.S. *Battler*, acrylic on paper

THE LOSS OF H.M.S. *BARHAM* AND A TALE OF WITCHCRAFT

On 25 November 1941, H.M.S. *Barham* in concert with her sister ships, *Queen Elizabeth* and *Valiant* and eight destroyers were covering an operation against an Axis convoy bound for Benghazi. On board H.M.S. *Valiant* was John Turner, a cinematographer and naval war correspondent. He had been filming the voyage and on that afternoon he was relaxing on the bridge of the ship when the German submarine U.331 penetrated the destroyer screen and fired three torpedoes into H.M.S. *Barham*.

The old ship, tough though she was, could not survive such a blow and very soon she began to list alarmingly. Turner picked up his camera and with two minutes of film left in it, focused on the dying ship. As H.M.S. *Barham* turned on her beam ends, her magazines detonated blowing the ship to smithereens. This terrible event was caught on film, in a few frames, the moment when 862 men and a proud old ship perished.

The Commander in Chief, Admiral Sir Andrew Cunningham was aboard his flagship, *Queen Elizabeth* and witnessed the scene, in his understated words "It was a horrible and awe-inspiring spectacle". He immediately impounded the film and a news blackout covered the whole event. Britain's morale was very low at that time of the war and the Admiralty and Cunningham did not see the need to make it any worse.

At the same time, a Scottish spirit medium Helen Duncan, resident in Portsmouth, was holding a public seance and one of the 'spirits' she conjured up for her audience was a sailor named 'Syd'. Syd had crossed over to the 'other side' that very day and as his image appeared, he was seen wearing his sailor suit and on his cap were the words 'H.M.S. *Barham*'. A relative of Syd's was in the audience and became visibly upset, nobody knew of his loss or that of his ship, no war office telegrams had been received by those whose loved ones were on the *Barham*, no information as to the loss of this ship had been released and when Syd's relative contacted the Admiralty, they were understandably concerned and contacted the police.

Before confronting Mrs Duncan, the police looked into her past and found that she was indeed famous within the spiritualist community, especially in Scotland where only that year, she had conjured up a sailor from H.M.S. *Hood* on the very day that the ship was lost. On that occasion, a naval civil servant was present at the seance and he was so concerned that he contacted the Admiralty at once. The Admiralty had not at that time been informed of the loss of H.M.S. *Hood* and told this witness not to worry. Within the hour they called him back and informed him that the *Hood* had sunk.

This was enough for the police who promptly arrested Mrs Duncan for being a spy. In prison she vainly protested her innocence and in reality there was no evidence to point to espionage, however the authorities still considered that she represented a danger to national security and had to find a charge to hold her. Eventually they found an ancient law dating back to the eighteenth century which had never been repealed. In what amounted to a kangaroo court, Mrs Duncan was charged and found guilty of the crime of witchcraft! The unfortunate woman was sentenced to 5 years imprisonment and only released when the war was safely over. The fact was that there was no rational explanation for her strange knowledge. H.M.S. *Barham* had been sunk and at almost the same time, Mrs Duncan had produced in front of an audience, one of her lost sailors. Although her activities defied explanation, the authorities had no doubt that Mrs Duncan was a strange personality with dangerous knowledge.

She may have been an ordinary Scottish housewife, she may even have been a witch but whatever she was, Mrs Duncan was a lady who knew too much for her own good.

H.M.S. *Barham*, acrylic on paper, 17 x 25 inches

MALTA

In June 1940 Malta was, to many in far away London, just a small island somewhere in the Mediterranean. Its significance in the larger scheme of things did not figure very highly in the minds of most army chiefs, licking their wounds after Dunkirk, or most airforce officers about to face their sternest test over the skies of southern England. Only the recently appointed Prime Minister Winston Churchill and the senior officers in the Royal Navy recognised the significance of this small island, sixty miles from Sicily with its naval dockyard. To Churchill, Malta stood at a vital crossroads of Britain's interests in the Mediterranean, protecting our oil supplies from the Near and Far East and keeping open the Suez Canal's vital artery through which these strategic assets would pass.

Churchill also anticipated that Italy would soon enter the war as a Fascist ally of Nazi Germany in order to pick up some spoils from the defeated French. In that very month Italy did enter the war, and Mussolini boasted that within three weeks his fleet would be riding at anchor in Valetta's Grand Harbour. In order to back up his words he immediately sent his bombers to attack Malta.

From this moment, Malta's ordeal would begin, it would last two long years, and expend much blood and suffering in order to ensure the island's survival and safety.

Each part of Malta's defence would turn into a singular epic. The only aircraft on the island were found in packing cases in the dockyard, four dismantled obsolete Gloster Gladiator planes, one of these would provide spare parts for the other three, and these three aircraft named Faith, Hope and Charity would pass into legend as they rose to defend the island against the massed Italian bombers, breaking up their formations and shooting down so many that the bombing offensive began to falter and Mussolini had to call on his German ally for aerial support. This duly arrived in the shape of the feared Fliegerkorps X, the most efficient ship-bombing squadron in the Luftwaffe.

The aircraft carrier *Illustrious* escorting one of the first important convoys to Malta, was marked down for destruction by Hitler himself. His instrument would be Fliegerkorps X and they went about their work with deadly precision, hitting the carrier eight times, setting her afire from stem to stern, but the courage of her captain and crew finally bought her through to Malta's dockyard where she was bombed yet again; but the gallant *Illustrious* survived to fight on.

Captain D.W. Mason of the oil tanker *Ohio*, a vital part of 'Operation Pedestal' a major effort to resupply Malta, was approaching the island when the first torpedo struck her, this would be the first of the 8 direct hits and 20 near misses this ship received on her passage. Her back was all but broken, fires raged almost out of control and her engines were dead, yet with two destroyers strapped either side of her, she made it to the dockyard and unloaded her vital oil. Captain Mason was awarded the George Cross.

Finally, and most importantly, the heroes of the siege of Malta were the Maltese themselves. 300,000 people crowded into a small island, they were subjects of the Crown and their reaction to a war that was not of their making was in June 1940, unknown, yet their courage and fortitude astounded the world. 10,000 of their homes in Valetta alone were reduced to rubble but they kept their island and its facilities going. They starved, suffered and endured but they never gave in. The George Cross they were awarded by the King now flies proudly from their national flag, a mark of their courage that will never be forgotten.

Finally, Mussolini's battlefleet was eventually moored in Valetta Harbour, two years after his boast, only now it was moored under British guns, surrendered.

Malta Dockyard, acrylic on board, 14 x 21 inches, bookjacket illustration for *A Share of Honour*, Alexander Fullerton (Little Brown)

H.M.S. *EURYALUS* 1941 British Light Cruiser.

Sister ships: *Argonaut, Bellona, Black Prince, Bonaventure, Charybdis, Cleopatra Diadem, Dido, Hermione, Naiad, Phoebe, Royalist, Scylla, Sirius, Spartan*

Displacement	6,850 tons full load
Length	512 ft
Speed	32 knots
Complements	480
Guns	10 - 5.25" DP (duel purpose), 7 - 20mm, 2 - .05 quadruple mounts, 2 - 2pdr pom-poms quadruple mounts
Torpedoes	6 - 21"
Armour	3" belt, 1" deck, 2" magazine

H.M.S. *Euryalus* was one of ten Dido class anti-aircraft cruisers designed in 1937 under the emergency rearmament program. The concept of an anti-aircraft cruiser was a new idea for the navy, in fact the only other ships designed for this purpose at that time were the American Atlanta and the Italian Capitani Romani classes. In order to survive in the battle line, a new type of gun had to be designed for these ships, a duel purpose(DP) surface and air mounting allowing for the highest degree of elevation. The American ships were armed with the outstanding 5" gun also employed on aircraft carriers, battleships and destroyers. The British opted for the heavier 5.25" mounting as used in the King George V battleships. Whilst useful surface weapons, as anti-aircraft guns they and their heavy turrets were somewhat slow to train quickly and the volume of shells they were able to put into the sky was less than their American counterparts.

However, *Euryalus* and her sisters were handsome well made and strong in spite of being somewhat cramped with five turrets on a short hull. In order to save space, the engines and ancillary equipment were installed in one large space and this did prove to be a problem when the ships were under attack; several were lost when torpedoes crashed into these large spaces and they quickly filled.

All these ships were extremely hard worked throughout the war, most of their service being in the Mediterranean under the brilliant command of Admiral Sir Andrew Cunningham. Used largely to protect the vital Malta convoys, H.M.S. *Euryalus* played an important role especially during the second battle of Sirte where she and the cruiser *Penelope* and a flotilla of destroyers under the command of Admiral Vian, beat off an attack on one of the Malta convoys by a much larger Italian battlefleet. She also shelled the Germans in Libya and the Italians in Pantelleria before helping to support the landings in Sicily and Salerno.

Finally, after returning to Britain for a much needed refit, *Euryalus* departed for the Far East to join the British Pacific Fleet in December 1944. Supporting the U.S. attacks on the island of Okinawa and other Japanese possessions and undergoing Kamikaze attacks in the process.

After the war H.M.S. Euryalus settled into peacetime duties back in the Mediterranean and the South Atlantic before being finally decommissioned in 1954.

At the end a long and useful life, *Euryalus* was towed away to the scrapyard in 1959.

H.M.S. *Euryalus*, acrylic on paper, 17 x 25 inches

THE SECOND BATTLE OF SIRTE 1942

The Second Battle of Sirte in the eastern Mediterranean on 22 March 1942, is a disputed event in naval history and has divided British and Italian historians as to who actually won it. It began with the passage of a vital convoy of four merchant ships to the beleaguered island of Malta. It was escorted by five light cruisers and eleven destroyers under the command of Rear Admiral Philip Vian. The convoy left the port of Alexandria and set course westward to Malta, intending to arrive in the hours of darkness in order to avoid the expected air attacks. The ships carried much needed ammunition, oil and other supplies and the pugnacious Vian was determined to see its safe arrival whatever the cost. And these odds were at this time against the British. Having had two battleships disabled in Alexandria by Italian frogmen, the balance of naval and airpower had markedly shifted to the axis powers. As the convoy sailed on it was detected by a German transport plane and soon a powerful Italian naval force left Taranto to intercept it.

When the two forces finally met, the Italians attacked from the north with two heavy cruisers and two destroyers. Vian ordered the convoy southward under a huge smoke screen whilst the cruisers *Cleopatra* and *Euryalus* lunged at the enemy. The Italians retreated but soon returned, this time in concert with the 35,999 ton battleship *Littorio* and several more destroyers. A furious gun battle developed as the Italians tried to head off the convoy at the edge of its smoke screen. The destroyers *Havock* and *Kingston* were severely damaged by the enemy battleship but Vian's ships kept up the attack in a now desperate situation. At last, the Italians could see the southward fleeing convoy and were moving in to destroy it. At this moment of gravest danger, the cruisers *Penelope* and *Euryalus* charged out of the smoke and made straight for the Italian battle line, guns blazing whilst the destroyers launched shoals of torpedoes. The audacity of this attack and the failing light caused the Italians to break off the action and retreat northwards. The convoy seemed to have been saved but by pushing the convoy further southwards the Italians denied it the possibility of reaching Malta under the safety of darkness. Inspite of heroic efforts, the convoy arrived off Malta at dawn and was instantly attacked by German and Italian aircraft. All the ships were lost with their valuable cargoes.

In spite of the tenacity and aggression of the Royal Navy which won them a well-earned tactical victory on the high seas, the object of all their efforts, the convoy, was ultimately lost because of the almost total lack of air cover over Malta itself. The incredible heroism of the Royal Navy was not enough to ensure the vital convoy's safety and thus the strategic victory was passed temporarily to the Germans and Italians.

H.M.S. *Penelope* and H.M.S. *Euryalus* open fire on the Italian Fleet at the second Battle of Sirte, 1942. *(Collection of Dan S. Somekh)*

K.M. *TIRPITZ* 1941 German Battleship

Sister ship: *Bismarck*

Displacement	50,950 tons full load
Length	823 ft
Speed	30 knots
Complement	2,300
Guns	8 - 15", 12 - 5.9", 16 - 4.1", 16 - 37mm AA
Torpedo tubes	8 - 21"
Aircraft	4 -6
Armour	12.6" belt

When the battleship *Bismarck* was launched there was some disappointment in German naval circles that she had been named after the 'Iron Chancellor' whose continental ambitions were matched by his almost total lack of interest in a German navy.

On the other hand, her sistership was named for the creator of the modern German fleet, Admiral Alfred von Tirpitz. However this ship with her proud nautical name was, unlike the *Bismarck*, famous for doing almost nothing. Yet, this inactive ship was responsible for tying down large Royal Navy resources, effectively denying these resources to the critical Mediterranean theatre and the Far East. The threat to the vital Russian convoys resulted in many of these being unable to sail and one, PQ17 was forced to scatter resulting in its almost total destruction by aircraft and submarines due to an erroneous signal that the *Tirpitz* had emerged from her Norwegian lair.

Although designed as a surface raider, *Tirpitz* was commissioned at a time when, with the loss of the *Bismarck* and *Graf Spee* and the neutralisation of the *Scharnhorst* and *Gneisenau*, it had become obvious that the days of the surface raider were over. This effectively left this powerful warship without a role until Hitler found one for her. By 1942, he had become obsessed with the idea that the Allies would launch a second front in Norway so he sent his most powerful warships including *Tirpitz* northwards to deter such allied action and to threaten the Russian convoys.

After arriving in Norway, *Tirpitz* only made one sortie to attack the virtually deserted island of Spitsbergen in order to deny its use as a radio and coaling station to the Allies.

However as long as she lived the 'Lonely Queen of the North' would always present a threat and the British were determined upon her destruction by any means possible. Firstly, R.A.F. bombers at the extremes of their range

unsuccessfully attacked the *Tirpitz*. Flying through a fearsome flak barrage, they were frustrated by the blanket of artificial fog generated by specialist teams on the shore and barges surrounding the battleship. The next attack came from the sea, or at least from under it in the form of midget submarines called X Craft which with incredible bravery managed to lay charges under the *Tirpitz* before their crews were captured. The Germans desperately tried to pull the great ship away from the mines but the charges exploded before this could be accomplished and the ship was severely damaged. The repairs took nearly nine months to complete and as soon as this was done, planes from the Fleet Air Arm swooped in and rained bombs down upon the *Tirpitz*, at least twelve hit and several near misses once again badly damaged the ship, but as no bombs had penetrated below decks the damage was relatively easy to repair and within another few months the battered *Tirpitz* was functioning again. Several more Fleet Air Arm attacks were carried out but the flak and smoke continued to frustrate them.

Now it was the turn of the R.A.F. heavy bombers to return, this time armed with a new special weapon, an 'Earthquake' bomb. Designed by Dr Barnes Wallis of Dam Busters bouncing bomb fame, his new creation was a huge streamlined 12,000lb device which was designed to hit its target at supersonic speed. As the bombers approached, the inevitable artificial fog covered the ship and they had to bomb blind. However one bomb struck the bow passing straight through the ship before exploding and causing a great deal more damage. By now the *Tirpitz* was hardly seaworthy and could only function as a huge floating anti-aircraft battery.

Most of the crew were bought ashore and the ship was moved to a new anchorage within the fjord. *Tirpitz* had been effectively neutralised but the R.A.F. hadn't finished with her yet and on the morning of 12 November 1944,

K.M. *Tirpitz*, bookjacket illustration for *The Gatecrashers*, Alexander Fullerton (Little Brown)

massed bombers armed with their huge bombs appeared over the anchorage, the smoke failed and the Luftwaffe which were there to protect the *Tirpitz* did not to arrive in time. With near perfect visibility the bombs rained down and two of them struck the battleship, blowing one of the forward turrets to bits and tearing a huge hole in her side. At last, the great ship finally surrendered to her fate, capsized and sank.

The *Tirpitz* represented the last of the effective big ships of Hitler's navy and one of the last of the great battleships. Her end was not glorious but whilst she lived, *Tirpitz* exercised a compelling threat and an inordinate amount of effort was expended in her eventual destruction. As a fighting ship, *Tirpitz* hardly figured at all but as a powerful deterrent, the 'Lonely Queen of the North' played her part to perfection.

U.S.S. *ALABAMA* 1942 American battleship.

Sister ship: *Indiana, South Dakota, Massachusetts.*

Displacement	44,519 tons full load
Length	680 ft
Speed	27.5 knots
Complement	1,793
Guns	9 - 16", 16 - 5". 20 - 1.1", 18 - 0.5"
Torpedo tubes	none
Aircraft	3
Armour	12.2" belt

Battleships are the most dramatic, powerful and charismatic warships ever built, they exude menace and violent purpose, yet their design is both functional and beautiful. As their name suggests, they were literally 'line of battle ships'. The irony is that during the Second World War, they never formed a line of battle except during the action in the Surigao Strait during the Battle of Leyte Gulf. And further to this, they very seldom took part in the great battleship duels that marked the sea actions of the First World War. The famous *Bismarck* action, the sinking of the *Scharnhorst* and the destruction of the *Krishima* in the Guadalcanal campaign were not only dramatic but also unique. After Pearl Harbor, the nature of naval warfare had irrevocably changed, the aircraft carrier had become the capital ship and the battleship had become their escort, providing formidable anti-aircraft cover and convoy protection. As well as this, the Second World War was the stage for increasingly large and complex amphibious operations from North Africa to Italy and Normandy, and the island-hopping campaigns in the Pacific. The battleship's role in these operations was to provide fire support. Such was the career of U.S.S. *Alabama*. A real workhorse of the U.S. Navy, *Alabama*'s operational record included convoy protection in the North Atlantic before moving to the Pacific where her operational duties read like a roll call of all the major battles of the island-hopping campaigns, from Tarawa, the Marshall Islands, the Carolines, Truk, Hollandia, Saipan, Palau, Leyte Gulf, Okinawa and Japan itself, the U.S.S. *Alabama* provided invaluable service and won many battle citations.

Strangely perhaps, the most severe test that *Alabama* had to undergo during the war was when, on 18 December 1944, her battle group was struck by an enormous typhoon off the Philippine coast. This disaster cost the Americans 3 destroyers, 146 aircraft, tremendous damage to 20 ships and 800 lives lost. Yet *Alabama* suffered only superficial damage and the loss of her three aircraft.

Following the end of the war, *Alabama* was placed in the reserve fleet and continued to serve until 1964 when after a huge subscription drive, she was handed over to her state as a memorial and museum and still serves in this capacity in the port of Mobile, *Alabama.*

And ironically it was here in 2005 that she faced one more great test when Hurricane Katrina hit the U.S. from the Gulf of Mexico. The old ship suffered some damage and took on a list, but all this has been repaired. One of the more inspiring sights of this terrible storm was a news reporter sheltering on the quay reporting the progress of the hurricane whilst behind him U.S.S. *Alabama* was taking the full force of the storm and coming through, still fighting.

U.S.S. *Alabama*, rides out the typhoon, acrylic on paper, 17 x 24 inches

JAPANESE SHIPBOARD SCOUTS

Owing to the vast distances of the Pacific, the Japanese understood the vital part that scouting aircraft would play in the coming war. Most navies carried aircraft on their cruisers and battleships but their use was somewhat limited to spotting the shellfire of their respective ships, and search and rescue missions. With the coming of radar, the U.S. and British navies gradually relinquished their shipboard aircraft and their consequent volatile petrol stores.

The Japanese, without the sophisticated radar of their enemies, relied on aircraft principally for scouting purposes and in this role, they were remarkably effective.

Most important fleet actions in the Pacific usually began with one of these scouts droning high above their enemy's warships, relaying their position back to their own ships. From Pearl Harbor to the very end of the war, the Japanese shipboard floatplanes and shore-based flying boats quietly got on with their work, and their value was acknowledged with the construction of the *Chikuma* (pictured here) and *Tone* as purpose-built aircraft scouting cruisers.

One of the problems the Americans had was the naming of Japanese aircraft of all types. The Japanese themselves tended to designate their aircraft either with a bewildering array of letters and numerals or poetic and symbolic names, thus the Aichi E16A1 became the 'Auspicious Cloud', whilst the Aichi M6A1 gloried in the name of 'Mountain Haze.

It is difficult to imagine the warning a U.S. airman would have to call out if he was attacked by 'waves whose form resembles figures woven in silk'! The simple solution was to give these Japanese aircraft American christian names, thus all fighters and floatplanes were boys whilst all bombers and flying boats were girls. So, the 'Auspicious Cloud' became 'Paul', and soon the Pacific skies were full of 'Jacks', 'Oscars', 'Claudes', 'Tonys', 'Petes', 'Dinahs' and 'Emilys.

The principal cruiser scouting plane employed by the Japanese was the Aichi E13A1 'Jake' and it was 'Jakes' that roamed all over the Pacific, seeking out American warships and spying on U.S. bases. The *Chikuma* carried 6 'Jakes', and these were constantly employed throughout their ships' lives.

Ironically, the most famous Japanese aircraft of the war, named by the Americans 'Zeke', was always known to both sides by its more famous Japanese name - 'Zero'.

I.J.N. *Chikuma*, watercolour, 16 x 25 inches

U.S.S. JOHNSTON 1943 American destroyer

Sister ships: *Over 175 of this class of destroyer were built*

Displacement	2924 tons
Length	376 ft
Speed	38 knots
Complement	331
Armament	5 -5", 4 - 28mm, 4 - 20mm
Torpedo tubes	10 - 21"
Armour	0.75" belt

American destroyer sailors always considered themselves a breed apart, 'the tin-can sailors' were continuously in the thick of the action and their heroic deeds light up the history of the U.S. Navy, but there is one ship and crew that has a very special part in that history. On the morning of 25 October 1944, off the Gulf of Leyte, the exploits of the U.S.S. *Johnston*, her captain and crew were borne into legend.

The Battle of Leyte Gulf was the largest naval action in the history of warfare. It was initiated by the planners of the Imperial Japanese Navy following the landings of General Macarthur's forces on Leyte Island in the Philippines.

These landings, if successful would set Japan on the road to defeat and the Japanese knew it. They had planned for such an eventuality and calculated that they would have throw everything they had at the Americans in order to halt the American advance. Therefore in an operation that was as complex as it was risky, the American fleet would be attacked from three sides. A force of two elderly battleships and their escorts would attack from the south, a much larger fleet consisting of 5 battleships, including the mighty *Yamato* and *Musashi*, 10 heavy cruisers and numerous destroyers would advance from the north and fall upon the U.S. transports disgorging their troops, whilst to the north-east lay the carrier fleet of Admiral Ozawa. These carriers were carrying almost no planes but their role was not attack but as bait to lure the battleships and carriers of Task Force 38 away from the transports they were supposed to be protecting and allow the *Yamato* group to destroy the helpless transports. The unusual feature of this Japanese operation was the emphasis they placed on the impetuous nature of the American Admiral commanding Task Force 38, William 'Bull' Halsey.

Admiral Halsey was a brave and committed naval officer. Through many frustrating years of command, he yearned for the chance of a decisive battle with the Japanese navy, where, like an American Nelson, he would annihilate them. Halsey's great strength was his courage and bellicosity but these traits were also his weaknesses as a commanding officer, and his urge for battle could easily lead to him taking risky decisions. The Japanese planners calculated this and built this possible character flaw into their operations off the Gulf of Leyte. In short, they knew their adversary perhaps better than he knew himself.

The Southern Force was all but destroyed in a furious night action by the elderly veteran U.S. battleships so recently repaired after their ordeal at Pearl Harbor. The major *Yamato* fleet under the command of Admiral Takeo Kurita was relentlessly attacked by submarines and hundreds of planes from Halsey's fleet. The loss of three heavy cruisers and the battleship *Musashi* forced Kurita to retreat. Then intelligence reports of Ozawa's carriers 300 miles to the north-east were transmitted to Halsey and, thinking that his work on Kurita's battlefleet was done, he took the Japanese bait and charged off with the entire Task Force 38, its heavy battleships, carriers and cruisers, to do battle with Admiral Ozawa's empty carriers. This left Leyte Gulf completely unguarded save for three small escort carriers, three destroyers and several small destroyer escorts.

Admiral Kurita had only retreated to lick his wounds and under the cover of darkness he again advanced towards the beachhead and the unprotected American transports.

Off the beachhead stood the three small carriers of the support group, Taffy 3, under the command of Admiral Clifton 'Ziggy' Sprague. His group was there to support the troops ashore, his planes were not armed to attack ships, only

U.S.S. Johnston defends Taffy 3 from the Japanese fleet at Leyte Gulf (Collection of Dan S. Somekh)

Japanese shore defences. Anyway, he had been assured by Halsey's command that the main Japanese fleet had been beaten back and was in full retreat northwards. Escorting the little carriers were the 3 Fletcher class destroyers, *Hoel, Heerman* and *Johnston*.

U.S.S. *Johnston* was commanded by Captain Ernest E. Evans, a popular, hard driving and somewhat mysterious character. His rise to command had not been easy for he was of Cherokee Indian stock and in the racially divided America of the time, where non-white seamen could only rise to the status of waiters and cooks on U.S. naval ships, his career was somewhat unusual. When he became captain of the newly commissioned U.S.S. *Johnston*, he impressed on his crew that he would never run away from a fight, like his hero, the American revolutionary captain, John Paul Jones he would always be prepared to put his small ship in harm's way'. To this end he drilled his men hard and efficiently to such an extent that his destroyer was known as 'G.Q. (general quarters) Johnston' throughout the fleet. In spite of this, Evans was well respected and liked by his crew, they found him quietly spoken and approachable but there always seemed to be part of him that they couldn't quiet fathom. Perhaps this was due to his struggles to gain command, or his experiences at the debacle of the Battle of the Java Sea where he witnessed totally inefficient ships being slaughtered at the hands of the Japanese navy early in the war.

On the morning of 25 October as 'G.Q. Johnston' and the other two destroyers stooged around their tiny carriers, their crews must have felt very

Artist's original sketch for the painting of U.S.S. *Johnston*, pencil on tracing paper

much in the backwaters of the action, the Battle of Leyte Gulf seemingly taking place somewhere else.

Suddenly, enormous shell splashes appeared around the carriers. Without warning and completely undetected, Kurita's mighty battleships and cruisers surrounded by flotillas of destroyers were bearing down on them at flank speed. Without waiting for orders, Evans laid a smokescreen to cover the carriers as they broke away to the south, before plunging straight into the attack. Bursting out of the smoke, Johnston made straight for the onrushing Japanese launching a spread of torpedoes at them. Bracketed by shellfire, the destroyer disappeared into the smoke again before reappearing and having the satisfaction of seeing one of its torpedoes blowing the bow off the heavy cruiser *Kumano*. At this moment, three battleship shells crashed into the *Johnston* knocking out one of her engines. The carnage was terrible, the living picking their way through the bodies of the mutilated dead that covered the deck. Captain Evans had the shirt literally blown off his back, his body pitted by shrapnel and one of his hands mangled, but he held the bridge and refused all medical treatment. With all his torpedoes gone and at reduced speed, Evans drove his damaged destroyer on towards the head of the Japanese line, blasting away with all his guns and scoring hits on the enemy as they massed to deliver their own torpedo attack against the fleeing carriers.

Captain Evans' tactic appeared to work as the Japanese seemed to became confused by the actions of this tiny, courageous destroyer and launched their torpedoes too soon.

However, the American escort carriers were suffering terribly, one of their number, *Gambier Bay*, was caught by the heavy cruiser *Chikuma* which riddled her with gunfire before she finally succumbed. Even then the brave *Johnston* staggered on, firing all the while until one by one its guns fell silent. Suddenly the Japanese fleet began to withdraw, David had faced Goliath and won, but for Captain Evans and his crew there was no celebration. Surrounded by Japanese destroyers pumping shells into the stricken destroyer, she finally capsized. As the remainder of her crew struggled in the water, a Japanese destroyer past through the wreckage. The Americans expected their enemy to spray them with machine gun bullets but there on the bridge of the Japanese destroyer, in full dress uniform stood her captain saluting the gallantry of their opponents before following his comrades northwards. For those who fought in the Pacific war, such images of chivalry were uncommon to say the least, to the survivors of the *Johnston* this must of been one among many strange episodes that befell them on that terrible day.

Sadly, Captain Ernest E. Evans U.S.N. was not amongst their number. He and 189 of his men did not survive, but they had sold their lives dearly in the tremendous battle, a battle which was clouded by mistakes and blunders by the high commands of both sides, and it was so often the small ships and their captains and crews that paid the price.

Captain Ernest Evans was posthumously awarded America's highest honour, the Congressional Medal of Honour and U.S.S. *Johnston* received a special Presidential Citation.

In the roll of honour in the history of naval warfare, U.S.S. *Johnston*, her gallant captain and crew hold a very special place, above and beyond the call of duty.

U.S.S. *JOHN YOUNG* 1978 American destroyer

Displacement	9,200 tons full load
Length	564 ft
Speed	30 knots +
Complement	340
Guns	2 - 5", 2 - 20mm Phalanx CIWS.
Missiles	Tomahawk, Harpoon surface to surface, ASROC anti - submarine, Standard, Sea Sparrow Surface to air
Torpedoes	6 - Mk. 46
Aircraft	2 - SH - 6OB Sea Hawk, LAMPS 3 Helicopters

Among the last NATO cold war U.S. Navy destroyers, the Spruance class (named for the famous carrier admiral of the Pacific war) at nearly 10,000 tons apiece were more like the heavy cruisers of the last war, at least in size. Designed principally as anti-submarine warfare vessels, *John Young* and her sisters were criticised as being somewhat under armed for ships of their size, with two small guns placed fore and aft and a box of ASROC depth charge rockets forward of the bridge, along with hidden torpedo tubes buried within the superstructure and a hanger aft for two attack helicopters.

In fact the design of the *John Young* was more clever than it looked, being a 'Modular' warship, she was built to accept many different weapon systems as they came on line, with the size and weight margin to cope with these new weapons. Among the first of these weapons' upgrades was the powerful Tomahawk and Harpoon anti-ship cruise missile systems. These deadly missiles not only proved themselves at sea but on the streets of Baghdad in the first Gulf War. Now they are in service in numerous navies throughout the world including the Royal Navy. The anti-ship missile has taken the place of the heavy gun as the ultimate ship killer. The Harpoon and its brothers and sisters can destroy a ship with one shot, delivered with an accuracy only

dreamed of by the traditional battleship designers. As well as this sort of firepower, *John Young* was crammed full of the latest submarine detection equipment and the means to deliver guided depth charges to their targets.

U.S.S. *John Young*'s career took her all over the world from the far east to the frozen north, from the Persian Gulf to the South Atlantic. Although she saw little ' live' action, she was in the happy position of saving more lives than she took having rescued at least 454 Vietnamese boat people and capturing the oddly named *Forever My Friend* drug runner in the Gulf of Mexico, seizing 8 tons of cocaine, one of the largest drug hauls in history. For this and all her rescue work, U.S.S. *John Young* was awarded the 'Humanitarian Service Medal'.

Ironically, after just over 20 years in the U.S. Navy, U.S.S. *John Young*, in her day the ultimate anti-submarine destroyer, was expended as a target ship by a torpedo fired from a submarine; her back broken she was sunk off the coast of Hawaii.

Whilst not enjoying the most action-packed life for a warship, U.S.S. *John Young*'s career was marked by selfless devotion in the service of saving lives both directly and indirectly and many, many people owe their lives to that service.

U.S.S. *John Young*, acrylic on paper, 15 x 22 inches

THE FALKLANDS WAR 1982

In the early spring of 1982, Margaret Thatcher's government was widely regarded throughout the country as one of the most unpopular in history. Massive unemployment, an economic recession, coupled with rising prices and cutbacks in the Welfare State were the visible signs of a country that had lost confidence in itself.

In order to effect an economic and social revolution, Mrs Thatcher had driven a stake through the very heart of 'consensus Britain' and in the cutbacks the armed services were not to be immune. To this end the Prime Minister instructed her defence secretary John Nott to cast a cold, accountant's eye over defence expenditure especially as it related to the Royal Navy.

He duly drew up plans for massive cuts in the Fleet. One of the new small carriers was to be sold off, the older carrier *Hermes* was to be scrapped and a drastic reduction in the destroyer and frigate fleet was to be effected. By April 1982 these plans were ready for implementation.

Over 8,000 miles away in Argentina, the military dictatorship that had run the country virtually into the ground was now in trouble. The economy was close to meltdown, social and industrial unrest was manifesting itself in almost daily street demonstrations and a sense of panic began to grip the military junta. With no economic solution on offer, the President, General Galtieri, fell back on the one issue that he knew would unite the country behind his government, the seizure of the Islas Malvinas, the Argentinean name for the British Dependency of the Falkland Islands.

Although this issue had been a bone of contention between the two countries for many years, both sides had been content to observe the status quo. In fact the British had all but forgotten their tiny colony far away in the South Atlantic with its 1,800 inhabitants and their flocks of sheep. Even an ' invasion' of Argentinean scrap metal merchants on South Georgia seemed more like an Ealing Comedy than a real threat to Britain's position in the world. Mr Nott had already withdrawn the naval survey ship *Endurance*, which represented Britain's interests in the South Atlantic, on the grounds of cost. Inadvertently, this sent a signal to the Argentine government that the British were not interested in the Falkland Islands – and perhaps they were right.

With the arrival of the Argentine army in Port Stanley on 2 April, the joke was well and truly over and Britain woke up to find herself at war. Even then the British were uncertain as to what to do. Most people in country had never heard of the Falkland Islands let alone that they belonged to the United Kingdom. The situation was clarified when Mrs Thatcher sent for the First Sea Lord, Admiral Lewin, who in answer to her question concerning the possibility of retaking the islands, said that not only could they be retaken but a task force could be assembled and set sail within three days to do this. But there were risks. In fact the

risks were huge. Lewin calculated that the Royal Navy could lose at least half the ships available to carry out such an operation even if in the end they succeeded in their mission. And if they should fail, Britain's standing in the world would plummet and Mrs Thatcher's government would be thrown out of office. The odds for success were 50–50 at best. Mrs Thatcher made up her mind on the spot and three days later the Task Force set sail from Portsmouth, picking up more ships from Plymouth and Gibraltar on their way south.

The Task Force, commanded by Admiral Sir Sandy Woodward, took three weeks to reach the South Atlantic. During that time fruitless negotiations carried on at the United Nations to try and resolve the issue peacefully, but given the fact that whatever was agreed would involve one side having to climb down with a massive loss of face, such hopes of a peaceful settlement had little hope of success.

Soon the Task Force was under air attack and then the elderly Argentinean cruiser *General Belgrano* was torpedoed by the nuclear attack submarine H.M.S. *Conqueror* and sunk with a terrible loss of life. From that moment on the die was well and truly cast, the situation would be resolved by force.

The sinking of the *General Belgrano* created massive controversy which stills echoes in Britain to this day and of course cannot be forgotten in Argentina. The problem was that the politicians responsible tried to cover their tracks with positional charts and diagrams in order to explain away their decisions. What both sides to the debate failed to acknowledge, publicly at least, was that Britain and Argentina were at war over the possession of the Islands. The *General Belgrano* was a warship not an ocean liner and the duty of the combatants is to drive their opponents from the seas. The age old ruthless lesson was learned yet again, with the poor conscripted sailors on the *Belgrano* paying the price of their leaders' folly. Following the sinking of their cruiser, the Argentine navy never put to sea again during the remainder of the conflict.

Revenge was soon to follow when the destroyer, H.M.S. *Sheffield* was destroyed by a deadly air-launched Exocet missile, and other Exocets sank the cargo carrier, *Atlantic Conveyor*. As the British established their beachhead on Bluff Cove, the Argentine airforce fearlessly attacked the ships covering the landings. Under a hail of bombs H.M.S. *Coventry*, *Antelope*, and *Ardent* were all lost, and bombs hit almost every other warship present at Bluff Cove. Only faulty fusing of the bombs saved them from the sort of losses that Admiral Lewin had predicted.

Finally, following savage fighting and losses on both sides, the Islands were retaken. In the Duke of Wellington's famous words it really had been 'a close run thing'; the British were unprepared and had to become masters of improvisation both in material and tactics. Their ships had been designed to track and fight Soviet submarines and were not adequately protected against air attack. They

H.M.S. *Broadsword* on her way to the Falklands, oil on board, 24 x 36 inches

had no airborne early-warning radar coverage; the radar-carrying Gannet aircraft and their aircraft carriers (*Ark Royal* and *Eagle*) had been scrapped two years previously in order to save money. The British had to rely on American Sidewinder aircraft missiles as we had no close-quarters aircraft missiles of our own. The untried Sea Wolf shipboard missile proved to be a real success against enemy aircraft, but they continuously had their radar locks broken by other ships in the crowded San Carlos water off Bluff Cove. The shipboard Sea Cat anti-aircraft missile was too old and proved useless in combat conditions. Yet, through all this, the British armed forces prevailed because they practised the age old Nelsonian dictum of war, the application of deadly and at times ruthless force in a limited situation. As can be seen with the sinking of the *Belgrano*, the bombing of Port Stanley airfield, the attack on Goose Green and the SAS attack on Pebble Island, these actions never allowed the advantage to be passed to the enemy; the Argentineans were constantly wrong footed and this created a sense of inferiority

which it became impossible to recover from. But the risks were enormous and if the Falkland Islands operation proved anything, they again proved that defence cannot be bought on the cheap. Before the conflict, the morale of the British armed forces was at a low ebb. After the victory, that morale was sky high and this reflected glory elevated Mrs Thatcher into an impregnable political position for the next eight years. However, her cost-cutting defence secretary John Nott had obviously lost the confidence of the armed forces he was there to serve and he resigned shortly after .

Yet, ironically the most positive result of the Falklands war was to be seen in Argentina itself where the cruelty, corruption and incompetence of their military government was exposed and they were swept from office like the scoundrels they undoubtedly were. It may seem strange that through all the deaths and suffering that both sides were forced to endure, the salvation of a great South American nation will probably be their lasting memorial.

H.M.S. *YORK*   1985 British destroyer

Sister ships: *Newcastle, Glasgow, Exeter, Southampton, Nottingham, Liverpool, Cardiff, Coventry, Sheffield, Manchester, Gloucester, Edinburgh,*

Displacement	5,350 tons
Length	466 ft
Speed	30 knots
Complement	314
Guns	1 - 4.5", 2 - 20mm, 2 - Oerlikon, 2 - 20 mm Phalanx
Missiles	1 twin Sea Dart AA launcher
Torpedoes	2 - 3 tubes 12.75" anti submarine
Aircraft	1 Westland Lynx helicopter

By the mid 1970s, naval architects and strategists faced a dilemma. Ships could be attacked from the air, from the surface and under the waves. Added to this was the new terror of the sea-skimming guided missile. The problem was to design a warship that could defend itself and others from these multiple threats without breaking the defence budget. If you were the Americans, you could afford to build anything that could float and be large enough to take any fit of weapons. Their answer to this problem was to commission the Spruance class ships, a destroyer of cruiser-sized dimensions capable of accommodating all weapons upgrades with room to spare On the other hand, if you were the British, you have to cut your coat according to your cloth. The Type 21 frigates had powerful attack capabilities but limited anti-aircraft and submarine weapons fits.

The large County class light cruisers which tried to combine everything, had as their air defence the incredibly complex, clumsy and slow Sea Slug system, and the ships were heavy on manpower and expensive to run.

The answer for the Royal Navy was to commission dedicated warships which were specialists in individual forms of attack and defence and did not break the bank in the process. Thus the Type 42 destroyer was born.

Designed and built down to a price, these ships were dedicated anti-aircraft escorts equipped with the new, efficient Sea Dart system, a 4.5" gun and some anti-submarine weaponry. The first batch, comprising *Sheffield, Birmingham, Newcastle, Glasgow, Cardiff* and *Coventry* had short hulls and somewhat cramped accommodation which made them difficult sea boats, and soon stories began to circulate about the class being unable to carry more than one motor launch and one anchor, as more would compromise the stability of the ship. Although these stories may have been something of an urban navy myth, there was no doubt that space was definitely at a premium and upgrading the systems aboard these ships was next to impossible without some drastic redesigning of the hull. The next batch, *Manchester, Gloucester, Edinburgh* and *York* were already slated for this hull redesign, being longer and wider than their predecessors.

In addition to this, in the light of lessons learned in the Falklands where the *Sheffield* and *Coventry* were lost to missile and bomb attack, close anti-air defence was beefed up with the addition of the American Phalanx rotary cannon system. As redesigned, these ships overcame most of the initial problems but there is no more room for further upgrades and they are due to leave service as the new Type 43 destroyers of the Daring class begin to come on stream.

The new Darings are reported to be the best, most advanced destroyers in the world, large enough to carry any kind of weapon and with their 'stealth' features built into their hulls, they represent a real leap into the future. When the flags are finally lowered on the remaining Type 42 destroyers they will have served their country for 20 years, not always perfectly but certainly worthily and not without distinction.

H.M.S. *York,* acrylic on paper, 16.5 x 23.5 inches

H.M.S. CUMBERLAND 1988 British Frigate

Sister ships: *Campbeltown, Chatham, Cornwall*

Displacement	4,200 tons
Length	471 ft
Speed	30 knots
Complement	250
Guns	1 - 4.5", 1 - Goalkeeper Gatling gun, 2 - 30mm Oerlikons
Missiles	8 - Harpoon, 2 - 6 cell Sea Wolf launchers
Torpedoes	6 tubes
Aircraft	2 Lynx

The term 'frigate' used to describe a very specific type of warship, a fast scout for the main battlefleet and a commerce raider. When the destroyer and light cruiser took over these tasks, the frigate shrank in relative size and became a sub hunter and convoy escort. Maids of all work, the Second World War classic frigates were the *Flower* and *Buckley* classes of Britain and America respectively.

When the Cumberland and her sisters were commissioned, the frigate had grown again, matching and sometimes exceeding destroyers in size and equipment. When the first Broadsword frigates entered service they carried Exocet surface-to-surface guided missiles and the brand new Sea Wolf anti-aircraft missile. This weapon was an outstanding success during the Falklands war shooting down several enemy aircraft. As escorts to the carriers and liners, they were the ships of choice, the big ships drawing comfort from their presence.

Following the batch two designs, in the final batch three (*Cumberland, Chatham, Campbeltown* and *Cornwall*), the design was improved on yet again with the addition of a 4.5" gun forward and the Dutch-designed Goalkeeper Gatling gun for close in support. The Exocet was replaced with the Harpoon system (with a nuclear option if necessary) and a more comprehensive anti-submarine capability.

It could be said that in these final batch three ships, the Royal Navy has three ships in one, with a surface-to-surface weapons system, an anti-aircraft capability and a powerful anti submarine suite. In short, H.M.S. *Cumberland* and her class are certainly one of the most successful warship designs ever employed by the Royal Navy.

H.M.S. *Cumberland*, acrylic on paper, 15.5 x 21.5 inches

H.M.S. *IRON DUKE* 1992 British Type 23 Frigate.

Sister ships: *Argyll, Lancaster, Monmouth, Montrose, Westminster, Northumberland, Richmond, Somerset, Sutherland, Kent, Portland, St Albans*

Displacement	3,500 tons
Length	436 ft
Speed	28 knots
Complement	180
Guns	1 - 4.5", 2 - 30mm
Missiles	8 Harpoon launches, 32 Seawolf AA Missiles
Torpedoes	2 - twin Stingray tubes
Aircraft	1 Merlin or Lynx helicopters.

The Type 23 frigate was originally designed as a purely anti-submarine warship to replace the ageing Leander class. As usual in the cash-strapped Britain in the 1970s and early 80s, they were designed to be built down to a price. As a result their specifications bordered on the ridiculous having no means of self-protection, having to rely on the fleet auxiliaries they were meant to be escorting for anti aircraft screening. Fortunately before such nonsense was allowed to prevail, the Falklands war bought the MOD to its senses and the lessons learned were to be built into the new, recast designs.

In that war the Royal Navy had prevailed with guts and ingenuity to overcome the cost cutting systems built into their equipment. Now, these sailors had earned the right to be listened to by the politicians and the Treasury, and to have their advice and recommendations acted upon. As a result the Type 23 frigates that eventually emerged have proved to be some of the most efficient and adaptable frigates that the Royal Navy has ever operated.

Not only are they thoroughly equipped for submarine warfare with advanced sensors, towed sonar equipment and Stingray torpedoes, along with the latest Merlin submarine attack helicopters with fully equipped servicing hangers, but they also carry their own special Sea Wolf launching system comprising a cell of 32 missiles, vertically launched to clear the ship's superstructures before turning horizontally towards their targets, the whole operation taking about two seconds. This prevents any blocking by the ship whilst trying to achieve a radar lock, a common fault with the old system.

H.M.S. *Iron Duke* has so many automated systems that a reduced complement of 169 men and twelve officers run the ship. The design of these frigates reflect the latest thinking in stealth technology, from their ultra-quiet engines to the slanting of the vertical structures to create the smallest possible radar signature, some say as small as a fishing boat.

Finally the Duke class have taken the role of film stars, appearing in the James Bond adventure ' Tomorrow Never Dies' and the ITV series 'Making Waves'.

Not bad for, initially, a cut-price warship!

H.M.S. *Iron Duke,* acrylic on paper, 15 x 22 inches

A VISIT TO H.M.S. *CHATHAM* IN HONG KONG IN JULY 1997

In early July 1997, I had the very good fortune to be invited to Hong Kong during the week of the hand over to China by the ship's company of H.M.S. *Chatham*. The purpose of my visit was to paint a picture of the ship which would be presented by her crew to their popular commander, Captain (now Commodore) Chris Clayton who was coming to the end of his command.

Whilst I researched the ship and sketched ideas for the forthcoming painting, I was afforded the kindness and hospitality that the Royal Navy is justly famous for. Yet in that relaxed atmosphere the serious business of dismantling Britain's role in this last of her colonies went on and H.M.S. *Chatham* had a large part to play. Daily press briefings, entertaining visiting dignitaries and the storage of the impedimenta of Empire, including armourial crests, flags and files, as street by street, the British colony and influence shrank over that last remaining week.

In order to familiarise myself with the surroundings and the ship I set to and did a large sketch from the harbour. Behind me laboured Chinese workmen constructing a formal garden in time for the hand over. During that week I watched the progress of this garden as mud and concrete turned into a lawn with assorted flowers and trees. Day and night the work never stopped except when the workmen occasionally took a look at what I was doing. When I asked them what they thought of the coming change in Hong Kong, they just shrugged their shoulders. Back in England the press were screaming that a wave of Communist oppression was about to engulf the former colony, crushing these workmen and the 'swells' who inhabited the Mandarin and Peninsula hotels. These workers just shrugged their shoulders and told me that the hand over was for them just another day.

The negotiations with the Chinese officials were apparently a little more tricky, with few cards to play, the outgoing British Governor Sir Christopher Patten and his staff ensured a very smooth and dignified leave-taking, untainted by any controversy or rancour.

During that week, the Royal Yacht *Britannia* arrived. We were informed that the Royal Yacht would appear round the harbour's mouth at precisely 8.30 the following morning.

And at 8.30 precisely, the following morning she appeared at the harbour's mouth bang on schedule. As we watched *Britannia* being eased into her berth by tugs, I remember thinking how immaculate, gleaming, polished and antiquated she looked amidst the bustle of cruise ships, ferries and low flying aircraft that was Hong Kong.

All too soon my week was over. Two days later, the colony of Hong Kong was handed back to China. The British Press moved on to other stories, the 'swells' continued their cocktails in the Mandarin and Peninsula and the Chinese workers shrugged their shoulders and got on with their day.

However, I will not forget the kindness and respect that was shown to me by all on board H.M.S. *Chatham* and for that all too short week, I was proud and honoured to be part of their company.

H.M.S. *Chatham* in Hong Kong harbour during the handover to China, watercolour. (Collection of Captain David Dutton R.N.)

Preliminary sketches

On the following pages are some of the artist's preliminary sketches or 'roughs' prepared for the final paintings. Important for any artist, such sketches are vital to the accurate portrayal of individual ships, in setting the scene, for composition, and in order to capture the drama of a particular event.

S.M.S. *Goeben* arriving in Constantinople, 1914, pencil on tracing paper

H.M.S. *Lion*, pencil rough

S.M.S. *Scharnhorst,* pencil rough on tracing paper

Dear Dan,

How is the amended rough. I couldn't fire
the guns from the rear turret as the smoke would
interfere with the airplane - so I have fired B
Turret - I'm not sure if this works - I could
replace the smoke with another 11" splash behind
the forward turrets - what do you think?

Direction of Ship
and Turrets.

SMOKE FROM
DISCHARGE FROM
'A' TURRET

HARWOOD.

SUN

H.M.S. *Exeter* at the Battle of the River Plate, pencil rough on tracing paper

BIBLIOGRAPHY

BALLANTYNE, Ian, *H.M.S.* Rodney, Pen and Sword
BONNEY, George, *The Battle of Jutland*, Sutton Publishing
BRADFORD, Ernle, *The Mighty* Hood, Coronet
BREYER, Siegfried and KOOP, Gerhard, Von Emden zur Tirpitz, Wehr & Wissen
CAMERON, Ian, *Red Duster, White Ensign*, Futura Books
COSTELLO, John and HUGHES Terry, *The Battle of the Atlantic*, Harper Collins
CRACKNELL, William H. U.S.N., *U.S.S.* Tennessee, Warshipe Profile
GARRETT, Richard, *Submarines*, Weidenfeld & Nicholson
GIBBONS, Tony, *Complete Encyclopedia of Battleships*, Salamander
HORE, Peter, *Battleships*, Lorenz Books
HOWARTH, David, *The Dreadnoughts*, Time Life Books
IRELAND, Bernard, *Cruisers*, Bookclub Associates
IRELAND, Bernard and GIBBONS, Tony, *Battleships of the 20th Century,* Harper Collins
JOHNSTON, Ian and MCAULLEY, Rob, *The Battleships*, Channel 4 Books
KOOP, Gerhard and SCHMOLKE, Klaus-Peter, *Battleships of the Bismarck Class*, Greenhill
LOTT, Arnold S. U.S.N. (ret) and SUMRALL, Robert F., *U.S.S* Alabama, Leeward Pubs.
MALLMANN SHOWELL, J.P., *U-boats Under the Swastika*, Ian Allan
MARCH, Edgar J., *British Destroyers*, Seeley Service
MASSEY, Robert K., *Castles of Steel*, Pimlico
PARKES, Dr Oscar, *British Battleships*, Seeley Service
POPE, Dudley, *The Battle of the River Plate*, Pan Macmillan
PRESTON, Antony, *Cruisers, an Illustrated History*, Arms & Armour Press
PRESTON, Antony, *Destroyers*, Hamlyn
RAVEN, Allan and ROBERTS, John, *British Battleships of WW II*, Arms & Armour Press
RAVEN, Allan, King George V Battleships, Bivouac Books Ltd.
ROBERTSON, R.G., *H.M.S.* Hood, Warship Profile
RUGE, Viz Admiral F., *S.M.S.* Seydlitz, Warship Profile
SCMALENBACH, Fregattenkapitan Paul, *K.M.* Bismarck, Warship Profile
SKULSKI, Janusz, *Battleship* Yamato, Conway
SKULSKI, Janusz, *The Heavy Cruiser* Takao, Conway
STEEL, Nigel and HART, Peter, *Jutland 1916*, Cassell
THOMAS, Evan, *Sea of Thunder*, Simon & Schuster
TONKS, Randall A.R. M.A., *H.M.S.* Exeter, Warship Profile
WESTWOOD, J.N., *Fighting Ships of WWII*, Sidgwick & Jackson
WOODWARD, David, Tirpitz, New English Library